THE
LETTER

THE
LETTER

MY JOURNEY
THROUGH LOVE, LOSS, AND LIFE

MARIE TILLMAN

GRAND CENTRAL
PUBLISHING

NEW YORK   BOSTON

Grand Central Publishing
Hachette Book Group
237 Park Avenue
New York, NY 10017

www.HachetteBookGroup.com

Printed in the United States of America

RRD-C

First Edition: June 2012

10 9 8 7 6 5 4 3 2 1

Grand Central Publishing is a division of Hachette Book Group, Inc.
The Grand Central Publishing name and logo is a trademark of Hachette Book Group, Inc.

The Hachette Speakers Bureau provides a wide range of authors for speaking events. To find out more, go to www.hachettespeakersbureau.com or call (866) 376-6591.

The publisher is not responsible for websites (or their content) that are not owned by the publisher.

Library of Congress Cataloging-in-Publication Data
Tillman, Marie.
        The letter : my journey through love, loss, and life / Marie Tillman. — 1st ed.
            p. cm.
        ISBN 978-0-446-57145-6
1. Tillman, Pat, 1976-2004. 2. Football players—United States—Biography. 3. Soldiers—United States. 4. Afghan War, 2001—Casualties. 5. Tillman, Marie. 6. Women—United States—Biography. 7. Widows—United States—Biography. I. Title.
        GV939.T49T54 2012
        796.332092—dc23
        [B]
                                                        2011020983

For Christine and Paul,
who remind me not only where I came from
but what I can become.

ACKNOWLEDGMENTS

Bringing this book to light has been a long and somewhat bumpy road, and without the encouragement, love, and support of many people it wouldn't have been possible. Thank you to my friends and family, who have seen me through the most difficult of times and have always been there to listen, give advice, or just sit with me.

Thank you to Howard Yoon for guiding me through this crazy process and believing the story I wanted to tell was worth telling.

I am forever grateful to Jenna Free, who spent countless hours helping me turn a bunch of scattered memories and stories in tattered journals into a book.

Thank you to Bob Free and Carolyn Corker-Free for the use of their beautiful Silica Ranch as a writing retreat.

Many thanks to everyone at Grand Central, especially Sara Weiss and Jamie Raab.

Thank you to the early readers of the manuscript: Athena Wickam, who has walked a similar path, your amazing spirit inspires me; Gina Hart for your lifelong friendship, diligent notes, and gentle but honest insight.

Thank you to my parents, Paul and Bindy Ugenti, for your unconditional love and support. Knowing you are always there no matter what has allowed me to soar. Thank you for your patience and for loving me enough to let me find my own way.

To my brother, Paul Ugenti, a willing travel partner who in the streets of Cambodia encouraged me to take the leap and has been cheering me on ever since.

Thank you to Alex Garwood for protecting me, carrying the heavy load, and granting me the time and space I so desperately needed.

To my sister, Christine Garwood, thank you for the endless phone conversations and a lifetime of unwavering encouragement and support.

And most important, to Joe Shenton, who in the midst of chaos just saw me. Thank you for your love and light, and for bringing three beautiful boys and endless possibility to my life. I love you.

THE
LETTER

PREFACE

Many people in my life were surprised to hear I was writing a book about my experiences. The person I was in 2004, when my husband, Pat Tillman, was killed, would be more surprised than anyone.

When Pat died, the media and the public at large became fascinated with his story. His image was everywhere, and it seemed like everyone had something to say about why he left an NFL career to enlist in the military in the first place, or what his death meant. His biography was told and retold; clips from his college and NFL careers were broadcast again and again. So much of his life was out in public, and the things that were mine—the details of our life together, and how I was coping with the loss of him—I wanted to keep close. I wanted to keep something for myself. I also felt fearful that if I shared my memories, somehow they'd evaporate. They'd float out of my mouth, into the atmosphere, and be gone. I'd lose them forever. My need to keep everything contained, to keep everything private, was primal.

In my grief, I shut out even my close family and friends. But one thing I did open myself up to was books. Reading other people's accounts of loss made me feel less alone, more connected. I could read from the safety of my room, where I could cry without fear that someone would hear or see or want to intervene. I underlined passages that spoke to me, then returned to them months and years later, only to find they spoke to me in a whole new way. The authors of these books, I realized, hadn't lost their stories by sharing them. If anything, they'd made them stronger by committing them to paper.

I understood what prompted them to write. I wrote, too, from the earliest stages of my grief. Most of it was stream of consciousness; nothing was crafted or polished, but getting the words down on the page allowed me a small measure of release. Unlike support groups, or even therapy, reading is personal, and so is writing. The combination was exactly what I needed then.

With time, I was able to go out into the world and connect with people again. I met veterans, widows and widowers, and people who had survived personal struggles—whether a death, an illness, or a divorce— who felt a connection with my story. I started to talk about my experiences after Pat died, and I found that other people took comfort in hearing what I'd been through. And it was healing for me, too—both to share finally and to know my story was helping someone else.

So though the person I was in 2004 would never believe she'd write a book, that's exactly who I'm writing for. I'm writing so that someone might open this up in the privacy of his or her room, start to read, and feel a little more connected.

Part 1: 2004–2005

It was good to be in Seattle—to hear the foghorns on the Sound, and the deep bellow of the departing steamers; to feel the creeping fog all around you, the fog that softens things and makes a velvet trance out of nighttime.

—Ernie Pyle

CHAPTER ONE

I leaned back in my office chair, staring at the account board and talking to my coworker Jessica about the day's business. We worked together at a consulting firm in downtown Seattle. At the end of every day, Jess and I would catch up and compare notes about clients and current projects. I liked her. She had a quick wit and a foul mouth—not to mention two perfectly placed tattoos: the first, about the size of a quarter, a series of concentric circles on the inside of her left wrist; the second, a row of alien-like dots that crawled up her spine, just high enough to peek out from behind a dress shirt collar. Jess was edgy but lighthearted, and made working in a somewhat uptight corporate office more enjoyable. After almost a year of working together, we had become close friends.

We sat there contemplating the idea of getting a drink downstairs to wait out the rush hour traffic, as we had done many nights before. Jess's drink of choice, Corona, no fruit; mine, a glass of red wine. The receptionist Ted suddenly leaned into my workspace. He looked at me and then let his eyes fall to the ground. It's an image I'll never forget—that pause as he looked for words.

"Um, Marie?" he said. "There are some people here to see you in the conference room...up front."

I didn't ask him who they were. I somehow knew. Ted was a big teddy bear of a guy who served as our gatekeeper, screening calls, protecting us. But this time I wanted to protect him. I didn't want him to have to tell me; I wanted to spare him. Or maybe I was trying to spare myself, give myself a few more moments before the inevitable. There was something in his voice and body language, or something waiting in the fear that is with you constantly when your loved one is in a war zone.

A chaplain and three soldiers in full dress Army uniforms were standing in the conference room when I entered. They did not have to say a word. I knew instantly that Pat had been killed. They had prepared us for this at the Family Readiness meeting a few months back. Class A dress uniform—killed. BDU, or battle dress uniform—injured. My mind registered their appearance.

Class A.

"We're sorry to inform you..." The words had no logical place to go in my head and ricocheted somewhere between hearing and understanding. The men stared straight at me, watching for my reaction—ready to catch me, I suppose. The chaplain pressed forward and took my hand. He started to pray but I cut him off. I needed to think, not pray.

Call. Call. I had to call my parents. I went over to the phone and dialed their number. My mom answered and I gave her the news. I shocked myself by how direct the words came out. There was no easy way to say it; the world as I knew it had ended. Pat was dead. Mom took it in for a few seconds.

"We're on our way," she said, and simply hung up.

I knew this would be her response. I didn't have to ask; I knew they would drop everything and come. That's why I called her.

I walked back to my desk in the stone-cold numbness of emotional shock. I picked up my purse and avoided eye contact with any of my coworkers. I didn't want to talk to anyone. I needed to get out of there.

Without saying much, the chaplain took my keys and got in the driver's seat while I walked to the passenger side. The soldiers walked to their cars to follow us home. They were all professionals. They had done this before.

As the chaplain drove, I stared out the car window, watching the scenery without seeing anything. It had been less than three weeks since Pat left for Afghanistan. As an Army spouse, you're given a rough idea of when deployments will happen, but the exact dates are never set in stone, and the schedule often changes. I had taken the day before Pat left off of work, expecting him to deploy that evening, but things got pushed and Pat and his brother Kevin, who had enlisted at the same time and lived with us, were headed out the following night. I had taken a lot of time off work and remembered thinking I couldn't reasonably take another day. Since they'd be leaving in the evening, it seemed sensible to go in to work for a few hours and come back in the late afternoon to see them off. Pat always tried to maintain a sense of calm before he left, never giving any indication that he might not come back or that our time together was limited. I woke up that morning and got in the shower, readying myself for a day of work. Once in the shower, I panicked. I didn't want to leave. What was I thinking? I didn't really care about this job. I couldn't leave Pat. So I called in sick and crawled back into bed, hair still moist. I woke Pat up as I snuggled back in, and he put his arms around me. He noticed my wet hair.

"What are you doing?" he asked sleepily.

"I'm not going in to work."

"Good," he said, and we went back to sleep for another couple of hours.

Now I closed my eyes as the chaplain drove the car south, from downtown Seattle to the little cottage Pat, Kevin, and I had rented in University Place. Snug on a hill overlooking the water of the Tacoma Narrows, it had been the perfect retreat between their training missions and deployments—a short drive from Fort Lewis but a world away.

The regulation twenty-four-hour cushion between notifying the family and releasing the information to the press had broken down, the officers had warned me. News of Pat's death had already leaked. I couldn't let his parents hear it first on TV or radio. I had to get in touch with them. I also didn't want Pat's mom, Dannie, to be alone when I broke the news. So with the chaplain driving, I made calls to family in the hopes that someone could get to Dannie's house and call me from there.

Just as I got home, my phone rang. I froze, looking at the caller ID. It was Dannie. This wasn't the plan; I knew no one was with her yet. I picked up and said hello. She was hesitant on the other end. "Marie, is everything okay?" No matter how hard my brain tried, my mouth wouldn't form the words. My throat closed up and refused to cooperate. Finally I just blurted out the words "He's dead." It was too harsh, but there was no gentle way to tell her. For a moment there was silence. The phone dropped to the ground and from a muffled, helpless distance I heard the shock of the news I had delivered play out. The most agonizing scream from deep inside drew out Dannie's next-door neighbors and I listened, unable to hang up, as Syd and Peggy rushed to console her. Finally Syd picked up the phone and assured me he would stay there with her. The worst part of my day was over.

I was still on automatic. I inherited my mother's blue eyes, fair skin, and long fingers, but from my father I gained the ability to maintain calm in a crisis. In my family, my dad was the chief master of levelheadedness; my sister came in a close second; then I took third. You would think we'd get our cool nature from my mother's Swedish ancestors, not my father's Italian, but sometimes cultures get confused. When a situation becomes increasingly emotional or tumultuous, for some reason I become increasingly calm.

More men in uniform started to fill the house. I didn't recognize any of the faces until finally Jess and another work friend, Megan, walked in.

Jessica and Megan were the two closest friends I had made in Seattle. The wives of the other soldiers were quite a bit younger than me, as Pat had been a much older enlistee than most. I found much more in common with coworkers, like Jess and Megan, and I was grateful on that day that I had them there with me.

Megan walked up and gave me a big hug. Without saying a word, she took charge of the houseful of soldiers.

So many men were in our house that night, talking in hushed tones, their boots echoing off the hardwood floors. I didn't know any of them. Whenever they spoke to me, I just stared at their mouths, trying to decipher their words—jumbled streams that made no sense. I played my role, nodding and agreeing.

The strangers shifted uncomfortably, looking around at photos on the walls and books on the shelves, aware they were uninvited guests in our home. Our sacred space, so carefully constructed and protected, was being invaded. I felt like the walls were coming in on me. I wanted to scream at them. I needed to leave.

It was late April but the night air still held its winter bite. I was dressed in a thin black sweater and pants, and the chill slapped my cheeks, making me conscious of the moment for the first time. The last several hours had been a blur of logistics and phone calls. Finally there was nothing left to do but wait. Jess sat down on the front porch and stretched her long legs on the stairs. She pulled out a pack of cigarettes and offered me one. I wasn't ordinarily a smoker but this was no ordinary day. I took one from the crumpled pack and tried to steady my shaking hand as I lit it. I sat down next to her, and in silence we watched our smoke drift up into the trees and twilight.

We looked over the watery narrows between the Tacoma mainland and Fox Island. Pat and I loved our cottage's location because the light on the water shifted through the morning, afternoon, and evening. It looked like a series of Monet paintings.

As the sky darkened, the islands and the Olympic Peninsula became purple cutouts against a red-stained sky. Passing boats left dark-ribbed wakes and silver trails.

The silhouetted spruce trees around us merged with the purple-and-charcoal evening.

It seemed like Jess and I had been sitting there for only a moment when I heard the rumble of a car turning into the drive. My parents and my sister, Christine, had arrived. Back in San Jose, they had scrambled to pack their bags, make arrangements for my sister's kids, and rush to the airport for the flight up the rugged coast. Now here they were. I hadn't even spoken to my sister that day yet wasn't surprised at all to see her arrive with my parents. Of course she would come, and of course I'd known she would. She put her arms around me and did not let go. Mom and Dad followed. The thing I remember most about their arrival was that almost no words were spoken. There was no need. Their mere presence had a way of putting me at ease.

With my family there, the soldiers' job was done. They could leave knowing I was in good hands. They filed one by one out into the night.

Then it was quiet.

I took in the silence for a few moments, staring at the door, which had finally closed for the evening. My parents settled into the second bedroom—the room used between deployments by Kevin, who would soon be rushing home from Afghanistan. My sister fell asleep on the couch. I went to my room, finally alone—deeply, finally alone.

I recounted the events of the day but could not put

them into any logical sequence. Everything was still un-real. Things I had heard or seen but hadn't registered were coming back to me now that I was able to reflect quietly. Had the officers in the conference room really told me that Pat had been shot in the head or had I imag-ined that?

I still was trying too hard to function, to be logical, to cope. I had not broken yet. I hadn't even cried.

Wrapped in a thick comforter in our bed, I lay awake, curled on my side, staring at the wall. A small crack in the blinds let in a faint beam of light from the streetlamp below, and Mc, our orange-and-white tabby, flopped up on the bed, looking for a warm place to sleep. He circled himself twice, then nestled into the crook behind my knees and began kneading the blanket and purring softly. If I closed my eyes, I could pretend it was like any other night, but I couldn't close my eyes. I was trying to make some sense of anything. I gave up on sleep and switched on the small bedside lamp, which cast a warm glow on the room. I pulled my feet from under the covers, barely disturbing Mc, and quietly went to the dresser across the room.

Under a stack of old receipts and cards, I found the slim white envelope that Pat had set there "just in case." It had smoldered there for almost a year. He had written it hurriedly during an earlier deployment, in Iraq, in a moment when he had thought he might not come home—a good-bye letter—and placed it on the dresser without ceremony during his break between Iraq and Afghanistan. I had noticed my name written neatly on the envelope and had asked him what it was. When he told me, in an offhand way, I wondered for a moment if I should open it then. After all, he had come back from that deployment. But his enlistment was far from over, and the subject just felt too big even to have a conversation about. So it had remained stashed in a pile without another comment from either of us. But we always knew it was there.

I held the letter in my hands and stared at it. It looked like so many letters I had anxiously awaited from Pat since he had enlisted, but I knew this one was different.

Nothing about the day seemed real except for this letter that I could touch and feel. It was both precious and awful—the last communication I'd ever have with Pat. I sat holding it for many minutes. Then I carefully opened the seal. My breath caught, and I paused another moment with my eyes closed.

I slowly flattened the letter on my lap. It had been so carefully folded. I pictured the slow, childlike way his oversized hands moved when put to a delicate task. It was one of the traits I loved most about him. The imposing exterior masking the most gentle soul. I recognized his familiar scrawl and smiled. I was ready.

I heard his voice as I read silently: *"It's difficult to summarize ten years together, my love for you, my hopes for your future, and pretend to be dead all at the same time...I simply can not put all this into words, I'm not ready, willing or able."*

The words turned my head inside out: If he couldn't imagine dying, it must mean he was coming back alive. My heart lifted. Crazy logic overwhelmed me.

The page was a mess of ink and scribbles, of words and sentences crossed out. Rather than throw the letter away, he'd saved it, his thought process transparent. I could see his mind wrestling, and even if it wasn't some perfect piece of prose, I liked it much better this way. Not perfect, but real.

Among the scribbling stood these sudden words:

Through the years I've asked a great deal of you, therefore it should surprise you little that I have another favor to ask. I ask that you live.

The tears I'd held tightly all day finally found their escape and flowed so fast I couldn't breathe. I found myself heaving with choking sobs, my body shaking uncontrollably. Like a child, I crawled into the corner, resting my back against the walls of my bedroom to make it stop. I tucked my knees into my chest for comfort, the rest of my body curling itself into a ball. I waited for the sobs to subside but they kept coming. I didn't want a world without Pat. I just wanted him back.

"I ask that you live." His words burned in my head as I read them again. *How could he ask this?* I

wondered. *I don't want to live. I want to die, I can't do it without you, you know that, you're the strong one, not me!* I silently pleaded with him just to come back.

He knew what he was doing when he wrote those words. He knew that my instinct would be to give up, that sometimes I needed a gentle or not so gentle push. He had challenged and pushed me over the course of our relationship, seen strength in me when I sometimes didn't see it myself.

I both cursed and thanked him, and in the end he won. As I sat huddled in the corner of my room, knees at my chin, sweatpants soaked in tears, I gave him this last request. I promised to live. I knew it would be the most difficult thing I would ever agree to do.

It was many years before I realized this final request was a gift.

CHAPTER TWO

Pat and I had been together eleven years when he died. But since we'd grown up in the same small suburban town south of San Francisco, it seemed longer than that, like he'd somehow always been in my life. Pat's parents, Patrick and Dannie, moved to Almaden in 1980 with four-year-old Pat and two-year-old Kevin. Dannie was pregnant with Pat's youngest brother, Richard, during the move. My parents, Paul and Bindy, had moved to Almaden with me and my older sister, Christine, in the summer of 1979, pushed by our expanding family and drawn by the allure of sprawling tract homes, good public schools, and soccer fields in every neighborhood. We settled into our new spacious house tucked at the end of a long cul-de-sac just in time for the arrival of my brother, Paul. The new planned neighborhoods buzzed with young families, and my childhood was filled with bike riding and hide-and-seek with at least twenty other kids on our block.

Between our siblings and neighborhood sports leagues, Pat's path and mine circled and intersected at various times throughout our childhood. When we were four, we played in the same soccer league and competed against each other. Although I don't really remember him from then, I was vaguely aware of the rowdy, blond Tillman boys. Pat's brother Richard played on sports teams with my brother, Paul, and ours was the kind of community where you linked everyone based on who their siblings were. You just knew who belonged with whom, which family had which brothers and sisters. By high school, we shared mutual friends and we often saw each other outside of school.

Pat was on the football team in high school and was known around campus for his cool self-confidence, apparent even in his quirky, individualist sense of style. He would wear clashing plaid shorts and tops, or T-shirts turned inside out (because he usually didn't like what they said, I later learned, although it was always beyond me why he didn't buy solid-colored Ts to begin with). Pat had an easy, comfortable way with the teachers and other adults around school, and I'd often see him chatting with grown-ups, completely self-possessed in a way that I wasn't. I was painfully shy, never raising my hand in class, and terrified whenever I had to speak in front of others. If given the choice between an oral presentation or a written paper, I'd always opt for the paper, even though it meant more work. And when a speech couldn't be avoided, I would over-prepare, write copious notes, and stand there holding them, shaking, while I spoke. But Pat had an unusual ease and presence in front of a crowd, even as a high school kid.

And that's how I knew he had a crush on me.

The times we ran into each other in the hallways or hung out in the same group after school, he said very little to me and acted shy. And that wasn't like him. Pat talked to *everyone*. There was something to the fact that he was different around me. But I was too shy to inquire further, and like most high school girls, my friends and I paid the most attention to the older boys. Girls mature faster than boys in high school, and this was certainly the case with Pat and me. But by our senior year, Pat had grown five inches and filled out to a muscular 180 pounds. While I'd always thought he was cute, I certainly noticed the difference.

Right before senior year began, a group of us played a game of capture the flag. The guys all wore camouflage, while my girlfriends and I wore shorts and T-shirts. Fueled by hormones, we chased each other around our high school campus that night, and somehow or another, Pat "captured" me. He held on to my ankle even though he didn't really need to for the game's rules. We sat watching the game go by, though it was hard for me to focus on anything other than the light pressure of his hand.

After that, we each let it be known that we found the other cute. Our "broker"—because every high school romance needs one—was our mutual friend Jeff, and about a month later, Pat asked me out. The night of our first date, I paced my bedroom for an hour before Pat was supposed to pick me up, getting myself more and more worked up. What should I wear? What would we talk about on the long car ride? What should I order for dinner that wouldn't get stuck in my teeth? Frustrated, I finally picked a simple outfit of white jean shorts and a deep blue long-sleeved thermal shirt. I checked my appearance in the long mirror behind my bedroom door. The shorts were a few years old and seemed too short now, especially from the back. Well, they'd have to do, I thought as I looked at the clock.

I quickly put on lip gloss and noticed that my hand was shaking. As much as I tried to maintain a cool exterior, my insecurities bubbled to the surface. Though no one—not my sister, not my closest friends—knew, I spent most of my days and nights filled with self-doubt. On the outside, I looked put together enough; my clothes, friends, and activities all indicated that I was a normal, happy kid. But on the inside, I questioned everything I did or said.

Just then, I heard the doorbell ring downstairs. Pat had arrived.

He was down in the foyer, talking to my dad, and smiled when I reached the bottom of the stairs. I quickly said good-bye to my dad and opened the front door so we could escape the parental interrogation. I was relieved that Pat seemed nervous, too, and he sweetly opened the car door for me. He had clearly put a lot into planning our date. Among our friends, no one went out on *real* dates; instead we usually hung out in groups or, at most, went to a movie nearby. But for the occasion Pat had borrowed his dad's car, which he stalled several times as we drove away from my house. Somehow, his effort and awkwardness put me at ease, and we talked comfortably during the rest of the thirty-mile drive to Santa Cruz.

We ate dinner at a casual restaurant on the water and talked about our mutual friends, the football game the following day, and the parties supposedly going on after the game. After dinner Pat suggested we walk down to the beach. The sun was low in the sky, and the air felt chilly coming off the ocean. We sat down in the sand shoulder to shoulder, looking out at the water as the waves crashed up on the shore. Without the formality of the restaurant, and with the daylight fading into night, our conversation became more intimate. Pat told me stories about his childhood and asked about mine. The Tillmans lived in a more rural part of Almaden where roosters crowed and wild boars roamed the streets at night. My family lived in a tract neighborhood where the only wildlife we encountered was the neighbor's cocker spaniel. Pat's parents encouraged him to explore the mountain trails that encircled their house, to fish along the creek, and to climb the oak trees that dotted their property. My parents always felt more comfortable when I played closer to home. They repeatedly warned me about crossing the busy intersection at the end of the street when I took trips to the drugstore to buy Lee Press-On nails and Sour Patch Kids. So while we lived only ten short minutes away from each other, our childhoods were very different.

Though nothing dramatic happened that night as Pat and I started to get to know each other—it's not like thunder shook the earth and we both knew this was *it*— as I look back, it's clear to me that our first date, as innocent as it was, started us on a path that would change both of our lives.

As Pat and I began to spend more time together, I grew to realize how completely different he was from me. What must it feel like, I wondered sometimes, not to care quite so much about what people thought? I was the "good girl," the pleaser, always doing what I was asked. Though Pat was polite and chatty with teachers, he was always trying to see how much he could get away with. He was constantly testing boundaries, getting into trouble for usually harmless stuff, and the stories typically made me laugh. He once mooned a bus full of cheerleaders who were on their way to a football game, and another time, our junior year, he and a friend threw eggs at a group of seniors from the school roof. Pat was also one of those kids who always found a way to wander the halls during class. It seemed like every time I left class to use the restroom, there was Pat, just hanging out as if he had nowhere to be, though I have no idea how he got away with it. I couldn't even fathom not being where I was supposed to be. I admired the way he pushed limits. His relationship with authority and the way he questioned everything was very different from what I was used to, and I was attracted to his attitude.

But when you're the type of person who pushes limits, there will be times when you push too far. This happened to Pat only once, and the lesson learned was so powerful it stayed with him for the rest of his life. Not long after our first date, Pat got into a pretty serious fight outside a Round Table Pizza. On that night, Pat thought a friend of his was being picked on, and—always one to avenge a perceived injustice—he entered the fray with gusto, without knowing it was really the other way around. I was there but was inside sitting with my girlfriends for most of the incident. When I came out, the scene didn't seem that bad—or even that unusual. I was used to witnessing fights, and usually they were fairly innocent and brief. This time was different. Pat had beaten a guy up pretty badly, although no one realized how badly until later.

The consequences of the fight were severe. Pat was prosecuted, had to stand trial, and was sentenced to spend time in juvenile hall after graduation. While people might have wondered why quiet, serious Marie Ugenti was hanging out with a juvenile delinquent, I had already seen that Pat was an incredibly sensitive, good guy. A lot of people, including my parents, didn't think a juvie sentence was appropriate for a fight, which kids got into all the time. My dad had known Pat since he played Little League, and knew that he and his group were generally good kids.

Pat himself took the whole thing really seriously, though. While he didn't talk much about the trial or his pending time in detention, he felt terrible that he'd hurt another person, and he spent a lot of time thinking about what had happened and its consequences. He started spending more time with me, and less time with friends who were prone to getting in trouble. While a lot of guys his age might have been flippant about the whole affair, Pat was not.

It's funny to think about the early months with Pat, because our relationship then is almost unrecognizable when compared to what it became. Most of the time, we hung out in large groups of people, going to the beach or someone's house, and I'd spend as much time talking to my girlfriends as I'd spend talking to Pat. But there were moments when I would glimpse a much deeper side of him, like when he would get sentimental about his family cat or show a tender protectiveness of his younger brothers. I soon realized that, like me, Pat had created an exterior that masked his inner self. He was much more sensitive than his cocky demeanor and bravado would suggest.

Pat's time in juvenile hall that summer changed him. It was a lesson in adulthood and the real consequences that can result from one's actions. As part of his punishment, Pat was supposed to do community service. The judge allowed Dannie to check him out during the day Monday through Friday and drive him to a halfway house, where he helped the staff with a variety of chores. Several times, she invited me to come along so Pat and I could spend a little time together in the car. The first time she came out of the detention center with Pat, I could tell he was trying to put on a brave face, but his eyes were red from crying and he was having a hard time composing himself. We chatted about inconsequential stuff on the way to the halfway house; then he was gone. A few days later I got a letter from him.

6-21-94

Hi dude. I apologize for taking a few days to write, there are only certain times we are allowed to. I try to work out during "activities," which is one of the times designated for writing. I figure you would rather me come back normal and not write, than fat and write everyday. I did a little "detail" (clean-up) so they have given me time to write.

I'm sorry I was all red eyed when you came today. I handle the whole situation fine in here, but when I get in my mom's car I get sentimental. So do not worry about me because I am fine. I am glad I got a chance to see you. Actually glad is really not the word but the less I think about it the easier it is. To tell you the truth, I can think about anything until I realize how it ties in with how much time I have left or what I can't do.

I feel like an idiot saying that I have so much time. Some of the guys, my buddy the crank fiend I was telling you about, have years to go. So I have it easy. Back to my buddy, though, he was actually a very nice guy. Luckily I was transferred out of that unit. I really did not like it in that room. It wasn't much bigger than this piece of paper and it was solid cement. Bear with my whining for a while, will you? I really was frustrated in there. I have never actually been in a situation where I couldn't do anything. I was trapped. I'll tell you the whole story later.

In my [new] unit, B7 (jail jargon), it is like a random dorm. All the beds are in one room and it has a surprisingly good atmosphere. The counselors up here are real nice in this unit. The kids are very nice too, because they haven't seen anybody in here my size, and white, in a while. I even got a pretty good workout today. It seemed to be more of a show—the whole unit watched me. I'm sorry to be so vain but I'm very thankful they are that way. They all leave me alone and let me do my stuff.

Hopefully I will be able to write more often. Sorry for the pencil writing but it is all they allow. I figured if I wrote in cursive it would look funny so I decided to print.

It feels good to sit here and write. I guess you don't miss something until they take it away (I'm referring to the writing, of course). I hope this whole ordeal is over soon so I can move on from it. It is now finally getting bearable.

Tell your family that I miss them and look forward to seeing them again. I really hope you are ok. You seemed fine when I saw you today so I won't worry. I've got three minutes left so I'll wrap it up. Good bye. Hope to see you soon.

Pat

It was difficult to see Pat so emotional, but I loved getting these letters, because they gave me the chance to understand what was going on in his head. Over the past year we had started to trust each other, to slowly expose the thoughts and feelings that simmered below the surface. In Pat I found a confidant. I felt safe sharing my dreams to travel and study art, though I knew my parents would disapprove. And he realized he didn't have to keep up his tough exterior with me. He could reveal his more sensitive, vulnerable side, and I wouldn't laugh. Writing letters, the way we did while he was in juvenile hall, made opening up to each other even easier to do. He was struggling; he'd never been away from his family for so long before, and on top of that, it was hard for him to lose his freedom so suddenly and dramatically. In hindsight, I realize Pat's incarceration that summer started a new phase of our relationship, one during which writing about our feelings became increasingly important. We would be separating in the fall, and letters would play a large role in the college years that followed.

———   •

During the spring of our senior year, Pat had decided to attend Arizona State on a football scholarship. I could have chosen to go with him, but I decided not to. I chose UC Santa Barbara instead. Some of my girlfriends thought I was crazy not to stay with Pat, but I took my studies very seriously and felt UCSB was the stronger school academically.

Actually, I'd been interested in schools even farther away. Each time I got a marketing packet from Duke or the University of Colorado, I'd pore over the pages, thinking about how exciting it would be to explore a part of the country so far from home. My parents were less enthusiastic about the distance, however, and made it pretty clear that wasn't what they expected. I wanted to please them, and part of me was also a bit scared to go too far away. So in the end, I applied only to California schools and ASU. With my choice of UC Santa Barbara, I would be only four hours from Almaden—still close enough to drive home for the weekend. And I would be only a short flight away from Pat in Arizona.

Neither Pat nor I knew what to expect once we were away at school. We decided to stay together, but made that commitment without really knowing what that would mean. I had no interest in dating other guys, but I wanted to experience college. I'd decided to go into freshman year premed, which meant I'd have a difficult class schedule that would require my full attention. In my heart I hoped that Pat and I would be able to stay together, but I knew I couldn't be sure. When you're eighteen, starting a new, exciting life of coed living and freedom from parental eyes, long-distance relationships don't usually work out. People may start college attached to their high school sweethearts, but typically these romances end by Christmas or summer vacation. But though we were hundreds of miles apart, Pat and I grew closer in college. The transition to life outside sheltered Almaden rocked both of us. All of a sudden, we were thrust into this wider world and felt overwhelmed. We found comfort in each other, not only in the steadiness of our relationship but also in the knowledge that we were going through the same thing. On the phone for hours, we'd talk about how homesick we were, the things we missed about Almaden, and how weird our new experiences were. Our writing got more and more intense and frequent. We relied less on our family and old friends and relied more on each other. We became coconspirators, each other's point person—the one we would check in with each day and the one with whom we'd talk over decisions large and small.

"I just got my class schedule," Pat said when I picked up the phone one day. He sounded agitated. As an athlete, he received all kinds of special treatment; he even had an academic counselor in the athletic department who chose his classes and offered guidance on which majors would work well with his training schedule.

"Yeah? How does it look?"

"They have me signed up for some sort of remedial math class," he said. "I checked with some of the other guys, and they're all taking it."

"Oh. And you don't want to?"

"It's not a prerequisite for anything," he said, "and it seems like high school math. It seems like a waste of time. What do you think?"

"I'd look into it," I said. "Don't just take it because they put it on your schedule."

"Yeah, I know." Pat really wanted to graduate in four years, or earlier, and for the first time was taking his academic career seriously. It was one of the differences I'd noticed in him when he was released from jail. He went to college with higher aspirations for himself than he'd had previously. Just the spring before, back in Almaden, he'd teased me for studying UCSB's course catalog because I'd wanted to have my path all mapped out. But now he wanted his path mapped out, too, and was looking for advice. We talked it over awhile more, and he ultimately decided to push back and take more responsibility for his course load.

I hung up the phone feeling satisfied. I got so much from my relationship with Pat, and I was happy when I could help him, too, even when it was with something small. His football schedule was pretty grueling and he'd sometimes leave his room as early as six in the morning to lift weights or attend a practice, and after classes and more practice, he wouldn't get back until eight at night. So most of the time, I would fly to Arizona. In all our time in college, Pat came to UCSB twice. It just wasn't feasible, either schedule-wise or financially. Though Pat was becoming known at ASU as a football star, he didn't have much money, nor did he have time to earn any. I, on the other hand, nannied and waited tables as much as I could to save up for airfare. Sometimes when I visited, I'd do little things like fill up Pat's gas tank while he was at practice, or buy him some groceries, which always made him mad. He was adamant about making things work on his own and sometimes had a hard time accepting this kind of help from me. I admired his independence, and it made me want to rely less on my parents for support.

Though he didn't have the money to visit or buy me gifts, his gestures were always meaningful. On our two-year anniversary, at the beginning of our sophomore year, he pressed a dried flower in between the pages of a letter he sent me.

10-1-95

Two years ago at this exact time I was as nervous as could be. Acting out in my head how the date was going to go and hoping I didn't make an ass of myself.

Luckily the date went ok despite a few car stalls and the lack of blankets. I remember the day like it was yesterday and I'm grateful for every day since. It is too bad we can't celebrate the way we would like, but there's not much we can do about that now.

I want to thank you for the two years you've given me. Though we have been apart for much of them I would not trade them for anything. I would like to say "who knew it would have lasted so long?" but I can't...I always knew. I wish we were together so I could show you just how much you mean to me. I love you.

Pat was so open about his feelings for me; he was so open about *everything*, and that made it easier for me to open up. He was the only one who knew how terrified I was of making new friends, and how nervous I got every time I went down to the dining hall and had to decide who to sit with. It was the first time I'd ever let anyone see so much of the real me. Pat knew me better than anyone, and he made it clear he wasn't going anywhere. He sometimes drew little comic book pictures of the two of us—himself buff, of course, with long hair flowing behind him, and me with big blue eyes. He would clip out newspaper articles he thought I might like, always letting me know that he was thinking about me, or that he valued my opinion.

Being part of a pair was still relatively new to me, and I took comfort in it. That sense of being connected to someone in the world made it feel less big and lonely. We were in it together, whatever "it" was. Pat leaned on me more and more when he was having a hard time. I knew he valued that he could come to me with anything and I would always approach whatever was bothering him in the same evenhanded way. Our relationship brought stability to his life, which was important to him—especially after his parents divorced during our junior year. It was a consistent theme throughout our relationship. Pat was full of life and energy and chaos and was constantly just out there in the world. But he really needed a calm, consistent home base, and that's what our relationship was for him. And he gave that same sense of grounding to me, at a time when I was entering the world beyond Almaden and wasn't sure where the ground even was.

———

When we weren't together, we threw ourselves into our schoolwork. We were eager to graduate early, and ultimately, both of us did. In that way, neither of us had the typical college experience, filled with hookups and wild keggers. It was easier to avoid situations that offered temptation, and since we each knew the other was approaching social life the same way, we never had jealousy issues. Well, almost never.

I was in a sorority, and we frequently gave parties and hosted dances. Most of the time I was happy to go by myself and hang out with girlfriends, but sometimes there were events for which I really needed a date, and I didn't want to miss out just because my boyfriend couldn't make it. For one dance, I asked the friend of a friend's boyfriend, and while it was more a matter of convenience than a date, Pat didn't like it much. He made sure he was able to visit UC Santa Barbara for our next dance.

Though I was happy he was coming, I was also nervous. I had two separate worlds—one in Santa Barbara, one in Arizona—and they were going to collide for the weekend. I worried that Pat wouldn't like my friends or wouldn't like their boyfriends. I worried they wouldn't have enough in common, as a lot of my friends dated agriculture majors or surfer types—guys who didn't have much to say about sports. I feared I'd have to take care of Pat the whole time and make sure he felt comfortable, which was undoubtedly what I'd require of him if our roles were reversed.

Pat stayed two nights. The first he slept in my room with my roommate and me. Since I lived in a sorority house and not a coed dorm, we weren't set up for male guests, and I had to sneak him into the bathroom to shower. He was laid back about the situation, completely unfazed. The second night, we stayed at the hotel in Ventura where our formal was held. Through the dinner, dancing, and partying, Pat handled himself perfectly. True to who he'd been in high school, he was able to talk to anyone; skater, scientist, sorority girls—it didn't matter. The whole weekend reminded me of the things I loved about him.

While my Santa Barbara world was all about sorority parties and premed midterms, Pat's world in Arizona looked very different. As his football career grew more and more successful, he was considered a player in the highest level of college sports. Late in our college life, I visited Arizona the same weekend as an agent he was considering signing with. Pat felt pretty sure he was going to go with him, but wanted to see what I thought. He was growing accustomed to the shiny world of professional sports, with its quirks and characters, and was surrounded by guys who were well versed in its protocol. But Pat liked that I wasn't. Down to earth even then, he wanted to make sure he wasn't losing his hold on reality. The whole scene was foreign to me, so my judgment would be pure. On top of that, I had no agenda whatsoever. By this point, Pat had a lot of coaches and agents and people involved in his life talking to him about what he should do, but they all had something to gain in some way or another. My motives were simply whatever made sense for him.

The agent took us to a pizza parlor and was, above all, very nice and gracious the whole evening. In the mold of his profession, though, he was also kind of slick. He called Pat "Patty," which I thought was amusing because no one—*no one*—called him that. At one point the agent brought up the details of a theoretical contract and remarked, "Now that's not funny money we're talking about here." I couldn't even look at Pat, knowing that if I did, we would both start laughing. Pat was still a kid— we both were—and yet we were navigating a world most adults would think absurd.

———

After we graduated, we knew Pat had a decent chance of getting drafted to play pro football, although it was by no means a sure thing. My parents had an extra room at the back of their house with a big-screen TV, so both our families watched the draft over at my parents' house as our future was decided for us. It was a weird experience. With Christine, her boyfriend Alex, the rest of my family, and Pat's all gathered together, and plenty of food in front of us, it had the makings of a party, but it also wasn't really appropriate to celebrate when Pat's name might not be called. But in the second-to-last round, Pat was picked up by the Cardinals. Everyone cheered, and my mom snapped a photo of his name on the screen. I felt really proud, and really happy for Pat. I loved to see his energy and passion on the field. I'd seen him go from a scrappy little corner during freshman year to a really talented defensive player. He dreamed of playing professional football, and everyone was proud and excited to see his dream of being drafted come true.

And now we could really begin our life together.

Once Pat felt secure that he'd survive the preseason chopping block with the Cardinals, we decided that I would move to Arizona, and that we would live together. While I had dreamed of exploring a new part of the country and moving someplace a little more metropolitan after college, I was also excited no longer to be long-distance. So I packed my bags and journeyed once more to Arizona, this time to live. Pat and I had built a solid foundation over the previous five years; now we were ready to see each other every day and figure out just how strong it was.

Almost immediately after I arrived, Pat and I fell into

a comfortable, easy life with each other. We settled into a small one-bedroom apartment in Chandler, not far from the Cardinals' training facility. It was a quiet life; though we saw other NFL couples sometimes, mostly we kept to ourselves. We had a favorite Mexican restaurant we'd eat at all the time, we'd watch movies, and we'd entertain family and friends when they came to watch Pat play. Since Thanksgiving falls in the middle of football season, Pat couldn't go home to Almaden, so we hosted our families in Arizona. Our first Thanksgiving, we had twenty family members over for dinner. I spent hours preparing the table, making my grandmother's stuffing and a gravy I was sure the Tillmans would like. Pat was a good sous-chef, following orders and chopping and stirring as the need arose. He and my dad carved the turkey. I was twenty-two and already felt fully domesticated.

Though the relationship made me happy, the first year in Arizona wasn't a great one for me. I loved the little details of our daily life and routine, and the fact that we got to see each other every day, but I was lonely. While Pat had team members to hang out with, and a whole group from college, I didn't know anyone who wasn't attached to him. And while he was intensely focused on his career and the difficult adjustment to playing in the NFL, I was directionless. I'd rushed to graduate from UCSB with a biology degree, but had second thoughts about medical school. Though a career in medicine seemed practical, it wasn't what I wanted to do; I still had dreams of working in a creative field, maybe something in the arts. But I didn't feel I could walk away from it; sensible people surely didn't throw away perfectly good degrees to go back to school in something else. Pat helped me strip away the "shoulds" and "shouldn'ts" so that I could come closer to the answer. "Figure out what it is you love," he always said, "and do that." I decided to chuck the biology degree and went back to school in graphic design. I eventually landed a job doing layout for the *Arizona Republic*, and while it wasn't my dream job, it felt like a small step in the right direction.

My overall unhappiness that first year simmered beneath the surface, only to boil over at seemingly random times. One night I was home while Pat went out with teammates, and I watched the early hours of the morning tick away, my fury and frustration building. Here I was, in Arizona for *him*—away from family and friends, tethered to the demands of *his* job, walking on eggshells whenever he'd had a bad game—and yet he was out partying while I stayed home. Where was the fairness in that? When he finally came in, I gave him the silent treatment, and was cold the whole next day. It wasn't until the following day that I had cooled off enough to talk like a mature adult. Pat didn't feel remorseful about his night out, and by then, I didn't really want him to. He was twenty-two, doing what normal twenty-two-year-old guys do. And while he could have been more sensitive to what I was going through, the real problem was that I couldn't find my groove. I had been anxious to graduate from college and start my life, but the real world turned out to be much different from what I had envisioned. I was working in a job that was only mildly fulfilling, living in a city I didn't really like, and struggling to make friends and find my way. This wasn't the picture I had for my twenties. While Pat tried to sympathize, he didn't really see my perspective. He was living his dream and thought we should enjoy his time in the NFL while it lasted. While I felt frustrated with what I saw as a permanent situation, he looked at it as one piece of the journey of our lives together.

I did have a few tricks to combat my frustration, and the most effective was taking road trips. I loved to explore, to walk or drive with the purpose of reaching a beautiful destination. I was so obsessed with road trips, in fact, that I suggested one almost every weekend of Pat's off-season. We would pack up the car with a few things and head out to explore some neighboring state or town. I loved the open road, the music, the anticipation of seeing something new. Pat was the ideal traveling partner, always up for an adventure or whatever I wanted to do. And if that wasn't enough, he would drive, too.

Having grown up in the mild climate of California, Pat and I had a hard time with the scorching Phoenix summers, and one of our favorite road trips was to the gentler climate of Sedona. With its red rock formations and transfixing beauty, Sedona always left me feeling reenergized after long hot days in the valley. A spiritual Mecca, Sedona has been a sacred place for the Indians for thousands of years, and you can't help feeling the magic in the air.

We often hiked the trails extending out for miles around Slide Rock State Park in Oak Creek Canyon. Pat navigated the canyon like he navigated the world, leaping from rock to rock, never settling for too long in one spot, keeping a playful yet determined pace. I, on the other hand, searched for the least difficult, most efficient path to make my way down without landing a foot directly in the river, all the while anticipating the pool of cool clear water, the prize at the end.

"The world belongs to the energetic," Pat often said, quoting one of his favorite writers, Ralph Waldo Emerson. While I lived on the fringe of adventure, drawn to it but timid and scared, Pat lived smack-dab in the middle of it, fearless. It was something I loved most about him, and I secretly hoped that by virtue of proximity it would start to rub off on me.

———

Time passed easily this way, through weekends in Sedona, Santa Fe, and San Diego, and even a monthlong trip to Europe. By his second season, Pat had begun to feel a little more stable in his position with the Cardinals, and bought a small three-bedroom house so we could spread out and create a real home for ourselves. Soon after moving in, we took a trip back to San Jose. As had become our routine when visiting home, we dropped our bags and said hello to our families and then headed to Santa Cruz. We missed the ocean.

On this trip, we had dinner at one of our favorite restaurants, then decided to walk along the beach and the rocks that jutted out to the ocean from the shore. It was the same spot Pat had taken me on our first date, and over the years we had gone back there many times. I remembered how young and nervous we had both been on that first date, but now there was an easy, comfortable flow to our relationship, an unspoken connection and bond that had developed over eight years together. I knew exactly who I was when I was with Pat. Sitting on the rocks with him was one of my favorite places to be.

"Look at those two—how cute." I pointed toward two sandy-haired boys filling up buckets with sand.

Pat smiled as the boys started arguing over who should fill the buckets.

"I guess I kind of took it for granted growing up that we could drive over here whenever we wanted," Pat said. "It'd be nice to move back here someday, or at least get a little beach house for the off-season." We'd had this conversation before. Having lived away from home for so long, we both felt a distinct pull to someday get back to the Bay Area.

It was January, but the weather was mild and the sun

warmed us as we sat perched on the rocks. As we got up to leave, I noticed a small red box sitting on the rock behind me. I reached down to pick it up.

"What is this?" I asked.

"I don't know, open it."

Inside was a beautiful diamond solitaire.

I looked up at him, surprised and speechless.

He took the ring out of the box and slipped it on the ring finger of my left hand. We had never discussed rings, or what I would want, but it was perfect. A simple round diamond.

"Is it too big?" he asked.

I wiggled my finger. "No, it fits perfectly."

"No, I meant the diamond. Is it too big?"

I looked up from my finger, a smirk on my face. Only Pat would be concerned that the diamond was too big. "No, it's perfect," I assured him.

After so many years together, it wasn't a complete surprise, but I was still taken aback. It had been a low-key, lazy day, and while we'd had a million small exchanges over the years that had somehow made it clear we'd spend our lives together, I wasn't expecting a proposal. But it was a perfect moment. And I had never been happier.

CHAPTER THREE

Three years after Pat's proposal on the beach, I found myself staring at my engagement ring, unsure of what to do. I'd slipped it on each day for years, and its weight had become comfortably familiar, the ritual of sliding it on my finger as habitual as brushing my teeth. I looked down at it for a long time, unable to decide whether to wear it and my wedding ring that day. Would people be looking for it?

It had been only three weeks since I'd left my office with the chaplain, and this was my first day back at work. I had decided in advance to treat the day, a Thursday, just like any other day. I would get up early, drive to the gym by my office before most people got out of bed, avoiding gridlock on the road, get to my desk early, and clear through my in-box. So far, it had been muscle memory in action. The alarm went off; I got up, pulled on sweats, and grabbed the bag of clothes I had packed the night before. I drove up I-5 through the morning darkness in silence. Listening to music was something I wasn't close to ready for, and I didn't want to listen to the news. The noise of the news had taken on new meaning after Pat's death and I needed quiet. I parked at my gym, barely exercised, then showered. I put on black slacks and a black sweater. Then came the part of my morning ritual when I usually slipped on my rings, and I stopped short. Should I wear them? I wasn't sure, and I wasn't sure if people would look at my hand, but I knew people would be looking at *me*. I grew up in a suburb small enough that if someone experienced something bad—a divorce, a death, anything like that—everyone knew about it. If you happened to run into the person at the super-market or coffee shop, you'd feel awkward knowing her business without having heard it from her. You might try to be discreet, but of course you would scan her for evidence of her misfortune. *"There's that poor woman whose husband was killed. What a pity. And she's only twenty-seven."*

What would people see when they scanned me? I was thinner, definitely, than the last time they'd seen me. Probably a little paler. I chose black because I felt like I needed to be completely covered and in black all the time, like wearing pinks and yellows would suggest I was somehow all better. Still, I rarely wore color anyway, and the black felt right. But my jewelry—what to do about that? I decided to wear the rings.

I didn't need to go to work yet and in fact wasn't expected back until the next week. I'd returned to Washington on Tuesday and had planned to spend the rest of the week alone, a state I'd rarely been in since Pat had died. It was natural for me to be alone, and I'd often craved that time in the weeks I'd been surrounded by family, surrounded by friends, surrounded by press cameras. I'm a loner by nature; I like my space to process the world around me, and it had taken so much effort to be *seen* so much I wanted to retreat for a few days. Still, when I was alone at home on Wednesday, it had been so quiet, and there didn't seem to be enough room in the house for me and all I had to think through. I needed a place to be. I'd called Jessica and told her I was coming back to work the next day. When she asked if I was sure, I knew I was.

The office had an open floor plan, and we all worked at desks grouped together, facing one another, with separators between them that were only about a foot tall. The idea was that the office would foster interaction and conversation, which it did. But it was also very exposed. There was no door to close, nowhere really to hide if I was having a tough moment. I walked into the empty room, grateful I'd beaten everyone there. My tidy desk was clear, save for a manila envelope marked

"Condolences." Jessica had gone through my emails during my absence and printed out everything I might want to read later so that I wouldn't be overwhelmed. My in-box would be a safe zone. But what about my clients? Would anyone assume I'd been on vacation and ask where I'd been? What would I say?

One by one, my colleagues trickled in and set about their business. They said "hey" to me, as they usually would, but not much more. I couldn't stand the look in their eyes when we made contact, the pity-filled glances from those who dared to lock gazes. But mostly, people were afraid of the raw pain so thinly veiled, and avoided contact.

Jessica finally came in, and she plopped down beside me. She looked at me hesitantly for a second, then said, "Let's go downstairs," signaling our usual morning routine. I grabbed my purse and we made our way down to the coffee shop at the bottom of our building for the coffee and conversation that had started our mornings together for over a year. Jess filled me in on the office gossip, intentionally talking over the very large elephant in the space between us. And I was grateful. I didn't want to talk about the past few weeks.

———

The days immediately following Pat's death had been a flurry of action and a flurry of nothing. My parents and

Christine stayed with me in our little house while we waited for Pat to be flown to Dover Air Force Base, in Delaware, from Afghanistan. Kevin would be flying back with his remains. Friends and family started gathering in San Jose, where we planned to have the public memorial, but there was no sense for me to go there yet, since I'd be flying to Dover as soon as the plane from Afghanistan was expected.

Pat's death had set off a media storm. Though he'd been a football star at ASU and then had grown to be a valuable player for the Arizona Cardinals, outside Arizona he'd still flown under the press radar. But when word got out that he had chosen to leave the NFL for the military, every media outlet wanted to talk to him. Though he chose not to grant any interviews, stories about his decision nevertheless glutted the press for a while. Still, that was nothing compared to the apparent interest in his death. Interview requests clogged our phone lines, and news cameras lined the street in front of our house. In full retreat, my family drew the curtains. Overstuffed gift baskets arrived from national morning talk shows, baskets filled with things like bathrobes and slippers, food, elaborate flower bouquets, and notes indicating interest in doing an interview. My home now had the sickly smell of too many flowers, which made me think of a morgue. In sharp contrast to the ostentatious bouquets, the simple tulips I'd bought to cheer myself up when Kevin and Pat had left for Afghanistan still sat in small bunches throughout the house.

My family and I sat around and stared at one another, not feeling like doing anything, but desperate for something to do. My mother busied herself making green tea, cutting up fresh fruit, and trying to get us to eat. She tends to clean when she's nervous, so my house, though crowded, was spotless. My dad paced a lot, the phone glued to his ear, his voice quiet and tired. Christine would come into my room to escape, and like kids, we sat on my bed staring at each other in disbelief. There were so many details I had to manage, and things I had to plan, that Pat was getting lost in the noise. Christine cut through all that. She just wanted to talk about him. She loved him so much herself; he had been in our family for over a decade. She didn't want to tell stories about him—there would be plenty of that at the memorial, and we weren't ready for it yet—but she wanted at least to say his name and reflect on the basic fact that he was gone. She became my refuge, the place where I could go just to talk through the chaos and feel connected to something stable. Because at that point, it wasn't real to me yet. It was easy to handle details and pretend he was just stuck on deployment somewhere, without believing the magnitude of the truth. Christine helped me face the reality. In our adulthood, our relationship had evolved into more than just the closeness created by a shared past. Some friends are like family; she was family and she was my best friend.

There was nothing else to do over the next couple of days but prepare to leave, so my sister started helping me pack. "What are you wearing to the memorial?" she asked while investigating my closet. I didn't really have anything. It was strange discussing this practical matter of what to wear. Pat was gone and I didn't care about a funeral dress, but I needed to get something. My parents, Christine, and I drove up to Seattle in search of an appropriate dress.

The second we got to the Nordstrom downtown, I knew it was a mistake. Stepping out from the protected space of our house was surreal. Inside those four walls, the world had stopped. Everything in my life had changed the instant Pat was shot, but outside, the world remained the same. Now, in this large department store, the other shoppers moved frantically around, grabbing at things on the racks, while I moved in slow motion. Other people's lives went on as if nothing had happened. The energy of it made me instantly nauseous.

Our family walked numbly through the busy downtown streets to the Banana Republic. My sister helped me grab a handful of black dresses to try on. I hated all of them but quickly settled on a simple black cotton sleeveless dress with a thin white ribbon around the waist. My mom, feeling uncertain what to contribute, said she was concerned about how little we'd been eating the past several days, and suggested we try to have a meal. We went back to the Nordstrom Café for lunch. It was a place I used to go for lunch all the time, but I now sat in the familiar dining room in a daze.

Our zombie-like existence went on for a couple more days, and then Pat's body was finally flown from Bagram, the base of US military operations in Afghanistan, to Germany, and from there to the military morgue in Dover. I wanted to get to Pat and Kevin as soon as possible and had asked to fly to Dover. The Army couldn't arrange this, but a television producer who I'd become friendly with over the years had heard about my desire to get to Dover and called on her considerable resources to help me find a solution. A kind man who owned a plane was a friend of hers, and he offered to fly me there. It was the first of many gestures of kindness from complete strangers who felt affected by Pat's death. My family dropped me off at a small airfield and I boarded the tiny plane. I'd never been on a private plane before, but I barely noticed my surroundings. When we touched down in Dover, a group of soldiers was waiting to pick me up and take me to the hotel, where I'd finally face something I had been both dreading and eagerly awaiting: seeing Kevin.

Kevin and Pat had always been uncommonly close. Dannie had often joked that Pat loved Kevin so much he married a female look-alike. Kevin and I had large blue eyes in common, a trait that made Pat—who had comparatively small, darker eyes—jealous. Kevin was constantly sketching and leaving around little cartoons and doodles and would always give his characters big blue eyes. In a way, their relationship was a lot like mine and Christine's. With my sister, there was never jealousy. She was bossy when we were kids, but I was easygoing and happy to do whatever she wanted me to, so it all worked out. It was the same with Pat and Kevin. All throughout their childhood, Pat looked out for Kevin, and Kevin worshipped his older brother. They had been rambunctious playmates when they were little and sounding boards for each other when they got older, and they always had each other's backs. Though both were great athletes, they never had a rivalry. When Kevin accepted a baseball scholarship to ASU, Pat was ecstatic to have him there. I'd go visit Pat for the weekend when both brothers were at ASU, and we'd spend most of our time at the baseball diamond, watching Kevin play a triple-header. Their closeness didn't really ever bother me. Perhaps because I had a sister I was close with, I just got it. And I loved Pat's loyalty to and support of Kevin. It was an attractive quality—sweet and completely true to Pat's nature.

When Pat decided to enlist, there was little question that Kevin would, too. And when Pat and I moved to Fort Lewis, there was no question that Kevin would live with us. Their closeness was one reason; the other was that if he hadn't lived with us, Kevin would have had to live in the barracks, and neither Pat nor I would have felt comfortable with that. The kids who lived there were eighteen, and Kevin was definitely older in every sense of the word. Pat was granted a housing allowance, because we were married, but Kevin wasn't, since he was single. So when I scouted houses in University Place, I looked for a home for our family of three.

From the moment we moved in, the three of us became disconnected from our previous lives. We were focused on being part of something that was bigger than us, this greater cause. Pat and Kevin went to Fort Lewis every day, but they had little in common with the younger guys serving with them. I was commuting to Seattle and felt out of step with that world, too. If a friend asked, "Hey, Marie, do you guys want to meet for happy hour Friday?" I'd think things like "Sure, Pat and Kevin will be back from their tour in Iraq by then, why not?" Caught between two crowds that felt foreign, we found it was easier to live in a country of our own.

When Kevin and Pat weren't away, we fell into a routine. We made our own little book club, determining to read the same thing and talk about it. I'd make dinner and we would sit out on the porch or around the coffee table and discuss whatever interested us at the time. Pat was always finding new topics to explore and loved to challenge those around him to do the same.

One of our last books was John Krakauer's *Under the*

Banner of Heaven, a true account of a fundamentalist sect of the Mormon Church. The three of us were sitting around, talking about religion, when Pat decided it would be a good idea to get his Mormon cousin on the phone and get his perspective. Kevin and I sat in the background, amused but not surprised, as Pat called Brandon in Utah. Most people shy away from conversations about religion or politics, but Pat sought them out. He was genuinely interested in understanding his cousin's beliefs, and he encouraged him to pick up Krakauer's book. He wanted him to read it so they could discuss it.

On Sunday mornings, the three of us went to a diner in Tacoma called the Hob Nob, which was popular with students from the University of Puget Sound. We'd sit and read the paper, talk, eat omelets, and drink coffee out of thick mugs. Whenever we could, we'd take short road trips, visiting places like the faux-Bavarian town of Leavenworth, where we drank beer all day, then stopped at a river on the way home so Kevin and Pat could dive in. We made a family holiday card, the three of us in front of a Christmas tree and a menorah. We all wore cheesy Christmas sweaters, including our cats. When Pat and I went away alone—just once, to Banff in Canada—we felt a little guilty about leaving Kevin behind and shopped for a souvenir sweatshirt to bring back to him. There were definitely times that I wanted Pat to myself, but I loved Kevin—both because he was so impossibly sweet and because I loved a man who loved him so much.

Military life was difficult, and Kevin and Pat just wanted to get away from it at the end of the day. And while Pat had me, Kevin was single. So I tried to be there for him, too, making his favorite dinners and taking care of him any way I could. And he took care of me, too. Before one of their long stretches away from me, Kevin bought me a goofy-looking metal cat with huge feet for the yard. "This is Rusty Big-Toes," he said. "He'll protect you while we're gone." Kevin often sent letters to me when they were deployed, telling me to stay strong and that they would hurry home.

———

When I got to the hotel in Dover, Kevin was waiting for me in the lobby. He looked pale and exhausted, and I knew he saw the same when he looked at me. We hugged for a long moment, but we didn't say much then, or at all that night. I stayed up until morning with Kevin in his room. Neither of us wanted to sleep, although Kevin did nod off at some points. Neither of us wanted to be alone. We turned on the TV and let *SportsCenter* or something like it fill the room with background noise, but neither of us was really watching it. There was comfort in just being together. Before seeing each other, we had spoken, briefly, on the night Pat died. After calling my parents, I asked for him first when the Army came to tell me of Pat's death. When I was finally able to talk to him late that first horrible night, his voice cracked on the other end of the line as he confirmed what I had been told. Pat was gone, killed in an enemy ambush. He kept apologizing, feeling somehow responsible for not keeping his brother safe. What happened wasn't his fault, and my heart broke at the anguish in his voice as he said he was sorry over and over again.

The day after I arrived in Dover, in some nondescript office on base, a very nervous military officer tried to explain to me that I needed to sign paperwork that would release Pat's body while acknowledging that not all of him was there. I don't know if it was the numbness or the sleep deprivation, but I couldn't figure out what the man was trying to say. Kevin was there with me, and when the officer became so jittery that he stopped making sense, Kevin stepped in and tried to do his job for him. "Marie," he said in a matter-of-fact tone. "Since Pat was shot in the head, pieces of his skull are missing. If you want to wait for the rest of him, it will mean staying here for at least a week while they do DNA tests."

Kevin and I looked at each other. This lifeless body wasn't Pat anymore. We agreed I should sign the release forms so we could make the rest of the trip home, where everyone was waiting.

On April 28, 2004, Kevin and I were booked on a commercial flight back to San Francisco. Kevin was wearing his dark green dress uniform, and the stiff polyester pants and jacket constricted his usually easy gait as we walked through the airport. People kept stopping him and thanking him for his service. He smiled politely, trying to hide the discomfort he felt from all the attention. Kevin and I were given first-class seats. Pat's coffin was in the cargo hold. Once we were on board and in the air, the captain announced over the intercom that we were bringing a fallen soldier home, and asked for a moment of silence. It still—*still*—hadn't sunk in that he was talking about my husband, that he was talking about Pat.

———

Pat's memorial was held at the San Jose Municipal Rose Garden, which had also been the venue for our high school graduation. It was May 3, a day before our second wedding anniversary. Two thousand people lined the stadium, and the service was televised nationally on ESPN. John McCain spoke, as did Maria Shriver, and a host of former teammates, coaches, and friends. Steve White, a Navy SEAL who Pat and Kevin had befriended, also spoke. He explained that there's little you can do in an ambush, short of taking the fight to the enemy, which was what Pat had done. He talked about how Pat had been awarded the Silver Star for bravery, for courageously distracting the enemy so that others serving with him might have a chance to escape. "Pat sacrificed himself so his brothers could live," he said. This was the most we'd heard about how Pat had been killed; all we'd learned up to that point was that he had been shot in the head by the Taliban during an ambush. I barely registered any of it.

Christine's husband, Alex, who had been very close with Pat, spoke soon after Steve. He poured a Guinness for Pat before making a few remarks. "There have been some extremely eloquent and powerful words said today about Pat Tillman the war hero, Pat Tillman the football player, and Pat Tillman the public figure," he said. "You know what, they're awesome words, and they're very, very much appreciated. But... for those of us up at the front, his close family and friends... we've lost our Pat." He went on to talk about the things only those close to Pat knew, like the way he would say hello to everybody while out running, the way he laughed at his own jokes and would say, "See? I'm funny," the way he constantly tried to improve himself and demanded 100 percent of everyone in his life. "Pat never told you what to do," Alex continued, "but he certainly helped you find your way, even when you didn't know you were lost."

I read all the memorial service speeches afterward but, truthfully, remember little from that day. I remember the thick hot air that smelled of grass and sweat, my black cotton dress clinging to me as the perspiration dripped down my back, the sound of bagpipes. I wore dark sunglasses to shield me from the invasive eyes of the crowd. Surrounded by thousands of people, I felt lost and alone. I wanted to run. I needed to get out of there. I couldn't wait for the day to end.

Surrounded by enormous photos of Pat on large easels, by cameras and hordes of people I didn't know, I realized that Pat was no longer ours, his friends' and family's, despite Alex's attempt to put everything in context. The media attention given to his life and death felt like a violation. Speculation about why he had done what he had and trivialization of our lives caused me to fiercely guard my privacy. I have been described as emotionally guarded, and this is pretty accurate. My trust and friendship is earned in time, not given out haphazardly. I have many friendly acquaintances, but a small select crew of solid confidants. I am often suspicious and cautious with people, and the aftermath of Pat's death made this trait even more acute.

Pat had become an icon, a cultural symbol. His life and death meant different things to different people, and their interpretation of him often was some reflection of themselves, or the selves they wished they were. Complete strangers mourned him, but they mourned the loss of something symbolic, while we, his friends and family, mourned the flesh-and-blood man.

After Pat's memorial, Kevin stayed in San Jose a few days longer than I did, and returned to our cottage in University Place after I'd started back at work. We had decided to keep the place, to keep living together, until Kevin's commitment ended the following year. I didn't know where I'd go, anyway, so I appreciated the time to figure things out.

Kevin and I went about our days like two shadows. I left for work before the sun was up, then returned around seven p.m.

"Hey, Marie," Kevin said when I came in one night. He was spread out in his usual spot on the couch. The TV was on, but he wasn't really watching it. He had a book perched on his knee.

"Hey."

"I made tacos, if you want some." It was his signature dish.

"Cool, thanks." I dropped my stuff in my room, pulled on some pajama pants, and went into the kitchen. While neither of us felt much like eating anymore, we still tried to maintain some sense of normalcy. All I wanted was to go to my room, to let down the face I put on for others and just be alone, to go to sleep. But I felt like I needed to put in some social time.

I made myself a taco and sat curled in the big chair in front of the TV while Kevin and I watched *Arrested Development* together in silence. I took a few bites, then set my plate aside. When the show was over, I was relieved. I could finally go to my room.

That's how most weeknights went. On the weekends, I probably could have stayed in bed all day. But I knew that if I stayed in bed, Kevin would worry. He would feel like he needed to do something about it. I knew Kevin was saddled with his own grief and I didn't think it fair to burden him with mine. Had I needed him too much, he would have gladly helped me carry the load, and that wasn't his job. The words Pat wrote to me before he died could have easily applied to Kevin as well; he needed to be free to live his life without my anchor. I loved him, and as his brother had shown me for many years, love is about setting the other free.

So I got out of bed, and Kevin got out of bed, each of us putting on a show for the other. A friend of Kevin's who played for the Seattle Mariners invited us to a game once. We tried to go and enjoy the game, but as soon as we got to the stadium, we looked at each other and agreed it was a bad idea. We weren't ready for the noise, the crowds, the stimulation. We stayed a few innings, then left. Going to the movies, too, seemed like it would be too much. But once we were out of bed, we had to do *something*. So we went back to the Hob Nob, ordered our omelets and coffee, and sat reading the paper, both of us on autopilot and not really wanting to be there.

One Saturday I came home from the market and Kevin had a big smile on his face. He had gone to the store and bought a big whiteboard and an easel, which he assembled in the living room. "What is all this?" I asked.

"We're going to do Words of the Week," he said. When Pat was alive, we had talked about doing Words of the Week, but we'd never gotten around to it. "So let's pick five words from the dictionary," Kevin continued, "write them up here, and use them as much as we can all week. Then we'll pick five more next week."

It touched me to see Kevin trying so hard to bring a little light to our life. I faked my excitement for our new game and grabbed the dictionary off the shelf. We flipped through, trying to find our first week's words.

"What about 'stymied'?" I said. " 'To thwart; stump.' "

"Oh, that's a good one."

We tried really hard to be less pathetic. But those first five Words of the Week sat on the whiteboard, unchanged, for a long time.

———

Over a month after Pat died, I got home well after dark. Kevin was waiting on the couch when I came in, and I could tell he was agitated. "You're never going to believe this," he said.

Try me, I thought. I didn't think anything could unhinge me anymore. What was left that I cared enough about to be moved by?

"They think Pat was killed by fratricide, that our own guys killed him." I was halfway to my room and stopped, dropping my workbag. It took a minute for me to register what he had said; then a wave of nausea came over me. I thought I was going to throw up.

"But they told us he was killed in an enemy ambush," I said, my mind racing back to that first day, and to Steve White's speech at the memorial. "Why would they lie?"

"Colonel Bailey is coming over tomorrow," Kevin said,

referring to their battalion commander. Kevin didn't have much information. He'd been called into his commanding officer's office that day and been told in an offhanded way, "We think that it might have been a fratricide, but we're investigating it." And that was all he'd been told. That didn't leave us with much more to talk about. I went to my room and closed the door, needing time to process the news.

When Colonel Bailey came over the next day, he wasn't dressed in uniform but in civilian clothes. He sat with Kevin and me in our living room. He grabbed a piece of paper and did a rough diagram of what they thought might have happened. In a confusing move through a canyon, the platoon had split, he said. One ended up firing on the other. He said they were going to do an investigation, and that there would be a briefing for the family in a couple of weeks. Kevin was inwardly furious. In the time since he'd returned to Fort Lewis, he'd worked alongside guys who were responsible for his brother's death, and no one had told him. I didn't share Kevin's anger at first. I was upset; it was an upsetting and confusing situation. But I gave Colonel Bailey the benefit of the doubt, accepting that they needed to complete an investigation before they knew what had happened.

Pat's mom, dad, brother Richard, and uncle Mike flew up to Fort Lewis for the briefing, which was held in a small conference room on base. We sat for three hours and listened to Colonel Bailey run through his PowerPoint presentation. All I kept thinking was *I can't believe they put together a PowerPoint to explain Pat's death.* It seemed so clinical and dehumanizing. And for the first time, something about Colonel Bailey's story didn't sit right with me. Pat's dad, Patrick, asked a lot of difficult questions. Colonel Bailey kept trying to placate Patrick with compliments about Pat's heroics but never really answered his questions. At the end of the meeting, we were given a written report. Nothing had been provided in advance so that we could ask more informed questions, even though Patrick had requested these materials. We left the briefing with misgivings.

Around this time, I read that there's a kind of grief called complicated grief, although it's hard to imagine any grief *not* being complicated. Complicated grief is often caused when a death is sudden or violent, or when the grieving process is interrupted by circumstantial factors, making painful emotions severe and long lasting. With complicated grief, you have trouble accepting the death and resuming your own life. In treating complicated grief, some psychologists have found success with traumatic-grief therapy, during which patients continuously tell the story of death to confront thoughts and situations they may be avoiding, and move toward acceptance.

Based on the information the Army had given me right after Pat died, I'd constructed the story of Pat's death in my head—that he'd been killed in an enemy ambush—and was coming to terms with it. I wasn't any-where close to healed, but at least I was coming to accept that he *had* actually died. But if he'd died some other way, this changed everything. If what they had told me at first was wrong, maybe the whole thing was wrong. Maybe he was still alive. I went to the only story I wanted to hear. I jumped directly to fantasy and denial. Now I needed somehow to find my way back to accep-tance.

After the briefing, Pat's family and I decided to pursue the circumstances of his death in depth, filling out in-formation requests and receiving binders and binders of material, much of it with blacked-out text, in return. During the next weeks and months, I started slowly to reimagine Pat's death. Part of me didn't really want to know about the details. Pat was gone. I needed to face facts and find a way to put the pieces of my life back together.

But another, more complex thread of my grieving process started to unwind that day, and it would take a long, long time before it was finished.

———

I don't like attention and prefer to operate under the radar, where few people notice. Even on my wedding day—unlike most brides, who relish "their day"—I squirmed under the focus of the guests and the constant photographs. Luckily, Pat was there to absorb the spotlight, as he often did, and I happily gave it to him. Since his death, the spotlight had been hard to dodge.

With so much attention focused on me, I felt fully exposed and violated. As a means of defense, I developed a distant, cool exterior, trying to completely mask my emotions. I didn't want anyone to see what was going on beneath the surface. While I mostly wished for the superpower of invisibility, or the ability to take flight to avoid an uncomfortable situation, or—better yet—the ability to spontaneously combust, this mask served me well for the season of smaller memorials that followed the one at the rose garden. While I appreciated the genuine expressions of love and adoration, I hated being on display and having to suffer publicly through the most private of experiences.

Everyone wanted to see the grieving widow, but I had taken pride in this most difficult time that I could maintain my composure and avoid a public show. My composure was also my one act of defiance. Everyone wanted me to break down, because they wanted the satisfaction of picking me back up. They wanted to feel useful. I wouldn't give them that satisfaction. Everything else was out of my control, but *this* I could control.

I quickly realized after Pat was killed that many people are uncomfortable with death. Some can handle the immediate aftermath, can maintain the proper etiquette of bringing over food and sending flowers, but few can handle the stark reality of loss. They want you to grieve an appropriate amount of time, then move on. At Pat's memorial, someone had said to me, "You're young, you'll find someone else." Another person had said, "Thankfully you had no children." Others would respond to the fact that we were childless with pity. Most of the time people didn't even catch the inappropriateness of their comments, but occasionally, after seeing the look on my face, they understood the error in their words. I soon realized I shouldn't take these things personally. At such painful moments, some people unknowingly project their deepest fears onto you, the widowed.

How different it must have been during the nineteenth century, when people properly understood mourning. Widows dressed in heavy black robes and veils, covering their swollen red eyes and thinning figures. They were allowed to mourn fully for four years, not expected to "find someone else" the day after the memorial. Today Western corporate culture dictates two weeks of bereavement. Death should be sufficiently mourned in this time; then it's back to work. Even after September 11, one of the most devastating days in our country's history, flags hung at half-mast at the White House for two weeks. Then, as a signal to the nation to "move on," they were raised to full mast.

I think it's our fear of loss that causes people to act this way. Seeing the bereaved is a reminder that things don't always go as planned in life. You *don't* have control, and inexplicably, tragedy strikes. Most of my friends—happy and young—didn't want to face the reality that something could happen to them, too. Somehow, acknowledging that something can happen seems to increase the probability that it will, and you don't want to jinx yourself.

If people don't avoid you, they want to *do* something. When people are sorry for you and don't see an immediate way to help (there are only so many casseroles that will fit in a freezer), they write a check. So much money came in after news of Pat's death broke that we realized we needed to figure out a place into which we could channel it. A group of family and close friends decided to start the Pat Tillman Foundation, though we didn't really know where it would lead. Pat's closest friends spearheaded the effort, seeing it as a way to take all the public fervor over his story and bring the focus back to what Pat meant to those who knew him. One of the first decisions was to work with ASU to start a leadership program in Pat's name. I was involved from the beginning but didn't have the capacity to lead any effort, let alone a nonprofit. No one involved in the foundation ever made me feel bad for not doing more. In a sense, it was also their way of doing something for me.

My family, too, wanted to do something, especially in those early days. I remember them looking at me helplessly, wanting me to go see a therapist, to take a pill, anything to make it better. I understood where they were coming from, but it wasn't where I was. The only person who could really get through to me was Christine. She had a way of meeting me at whatever spot I inhabited emotionally, never pushing, but also never acting as though everything was fine. It was the same way she was with her kids. At a small gathering we'd had to view Pat's coffin before the memorial service, Christine's three-year-old son had asked loudly why Uncle Pat wouldn't get out of his casket. Many people might have felt embarrassed by his openness or questioned the wisdom of bringing a three-year-old to such a gathering, but Pat's death was a huge event in all our lives, including my nephew's life, and Christine wasn't going to pretend like it wasn't. And she'd never pretend with me.

Other than with Christine, I often held my feelings close, even with friends and family. I felt disconnected from everyone, like I was isolated on an island of grief. People couldn't read what was going on, so they often made remarks and acted in a manner that was so out of line with my internal emotional terrain it only made me feel more alone. But I acted fine to gain the freedom I needed to mourn in my own way. I acted fine to break free from the stifling embraces and well-meaning but misguided advice. I acted fine and went through the motions of my life.

For the most part, that life was dark and sleepy, with a consistent mist that hung over everything. Some weekend mornings when I would wake up with the hours of the day stretching ahead of me, I would put on my running shoes and start wandering the damp streets by our house. On these mornings, I didn't have the energy to be with Kevin but didn't want to hole up in my room, either. I would wander this way for hours, wrapped in the haze, moving down the long trail that followed the shoreline. The energy required to move my legs dissipated the spinning in my brain. But I couldn't get out of my head long enough to find peace or clarity. The grief hung all around me like a thick blanket, insulating me from the rest of the world. My shoulders sagged under its weight. I welcomed this feeling. It comforted me and became the one consistent thing in my life, my steady companion. I embraced it, dove deep into the murky waters of sorrow, and swam around.

Chapter Four

Several months after Pat died, I checked my calendar in the morning and saw I had completely forgotten about a doctor's appointment I'd made for my annual checkup.

I had been to the doctor's office only once before, and double-checked the address before I left. When I arrived, I settled into a cramped seat in the tiny waiting room at the top of the stairs, noticing a disproportionate amount of expectant mothers. Many, haggard but happy, were juggling a toddler and a diaper bag.

When I'd been there before, the previous winter, it was because I was trying to get pregnant.

Pat and I both wanted kids, and if it had been up to him, we would have started a family right after we got married. We weren't around kids all that much, but Pat loved them. When he played for the Cardinals, he'd made a great effort to come to San Jose for the birth of Christine and Alex's firstborn, even though he'd had only a small window between his practice commitments. He loved signing autographs for kids after games and always took time to talk to them and answer their funny questions. Also, Pat's parents had been young when they had him, and he always liked the idea of being a young dad. And our lifestyle was very settled. We'd been together a long time, and though we were still in our twenties, we weren't out partying every night; we were home cooking dinner and watching movies. But at the time we got married, Pat had just entered the military. I knew those obligations would take him away much of the time, and I couldn't see being in a new place with a new-born, without him, without family, without good friends. I knew early motherhood was hard, and didn't want to make it even harder by adding isolation to the mix. So I said we should wait, and Pat agreed.

A year and a half after that conversation, Pat and I stole away for a long weekend to the Oregon coast. We spent a night in the sleepy town of Astoria, then another in Cannon Beach. The beach itself was as wide as a football field, and an enormous rock formation jutted out from the surf, attracting so many seagulls that often the rock was as much white as gray. Though Pat still had over a year left in his commitment to the military, the end was in sight. We'd gotten over the hump. After Afghanistan, there would be one more deployment, and then the remainder of his service would be stateside as they processed him out. Pat was starting to look ahead to football, and we strategized how he could spend the last few months of his service getting conditioned to play again. We also renewed our discussion about starting a family. Even if I got pregnant right away, there would be only a limited time when Pat wouldn't be around once a baby was born—and even then, he would be close, not off in a foreign war zone. What better place than this magical beach to start a family?

But I didn't get pregnant at the beach, or during the next month. After only two months of trying, I was anxious about our lack of success. The window before Pat would deploy again was closing, and no amount of cycle monitoring and counting had worked. So I'd scheduled an appointment with a doctor who might help or at least put my mind at ease.

Now I laughed at my former self, who thought she could control so much, who thought she could skillfully schedule a birth to correspond with a small window of time between Pat's multiple deployments. Everything had changed. No baby, no pregnancy, no husband, no control.

After I learned Pat had been killed, there was still a chance—though remote—that I might be pregnant. When I got my period not long after Pat's memorial service, I was disappointed, but too overwhelmed by everything else to really process it. *Well, there's that,* I had thought.

The doctor's assistant called me in, and I went through the motions of the exam. When my doctor was through, she asked me how I was doing. It's a typical question from a doctor to a patient. But as I started to give my automatic answer of "Fine," tears welled up in my eyes. A knot formed in my throat and I couldn't speak. Grasping at the flimsy paper gown wrapped around me, I felt completely vulnerable. For months, I had successfully guarded myself, but here I was, physically and emotionally exposed. Once unleashed, the raw emotion flew out of me. I shook, sobbing uncontrollably. *I should be able to control myself better,* I thought, humiliated.

My doctor looked at me sympathetically as I quickly brushed away the tears and struggled to put my clothes on. She pulled a small prescription pad out of her coat pocket and scribbled something on it. Then she handed it over and said, "Here—this may help." It was a prescription for the antidepressant Wellbutrin. I shoved it into my pocket, thanked her, and left.

On the drive home through the rain-soaked streets, as I got past my initial embarrassment for breaking down, I suddenly felt angry. I barely knew this doctor; I hadn't seen her in over a year. She knew I had recently lost my husband, but we'd barely spoken during the exam, and because I broke down in her office, she offered me an antidepressant, as if my display of emotion was something I should put an end to through any means possible. She didn't ask any questions other than "How are you doing?" And based on my response, she decided I clearly needed to be medicated.

I was no stranger to blue moods. Through my adolescence and early twenties, I lived stretches of time masking a low-grade, steady sense of insecurity and gloom. But I'd always found a way to break free. Because of this kinship to melancholy, I worried when Pat was killed that I would fall into a deep hole and never find my way out, but in the months that had passed, that hadn't happened. I was grieving, and this doctor wanted to throw medication at me to make it go away, as if it could. In a way, it felt like the same societal message: two weeks to grieve, then it's back to work.

As views of the narrows came into sight, framed at every angle by pine trees or craftsman houses, my thoughts continued, clearer than they'd been in months. I saw that the reason I'd been able to control my emotions for so long was that I'd been numb. The coma of sudden loss had lulled me into a false sense of control. Now, driving the side streets back home, I knew the numbness was gone. Grief, I then realized, is not something to be contained. You can try to lock it away, but it finds its way through the cracks and holes in our lives.

I was depressed, but my husband had just been killed and it felt like the proper emotion. I wanted to feel this pain deeply, purely. I knew medication was an option if things became unbearable. But for the moment, I could bear it and wanted to work through the pain in my own way. I just needed time and space to sort through all that had happened, not just over the past few months since Pat had died but in the time before.

———

It was only four years earlier, the fall of 2001, when Kevin had come to Phoenix for the weekend to see Pat play and visit a few friends. A small crew had assembled at our place after the game and sat chatting and enjoying drinks around the fire pit outside. After a couple of hours, I went to bed but lay awake listening to the low rumble of chatter, punctuated by an occasional laugh, coming from the backyard. The conversation quickly flowed from the game to the recent events on September 11. It was still fresh in everyone's mind, and they debated the conflicting stories already coming out of the tragedy. I was almost asleep when Pat climbed into bed. I folded into him and lay my head on his chest. A few minutes passed but I could tell his mind was still turning from the conversation outside.

"What if I joined the Army?" he said into the darkness.

I opened my eyes and saw the outline of his face staring up at the ceiling.

"Are you serious?" I asked.

"I don't know, maybe," he replied.

The words that passed between us hung in the air, then sunk slowly in. We knew there was more to talk about, but that was it for the night. The seed was planted in our minds.

We had both been affected by the events of September 11. It was horrible; how could we not have been? I'd gone on a run that morning before turning on the radio or television, and when I got back, Pat was watching the news unfold. Kevin had called and woken him up to tell him to turn on the television. I sat watching with Pat for a little while, stunned by the images but still not completely sure what was going on. Only later, when I was watching with my colleagues at work, did it become clear it was a terrorist attack. Pat watched alone for a while once I went to work, then left to watch reports from the Cardinals' training facility.

That night, we kept following events on the news. We didn't talk about it that much, just watched. While our sadness was the same, we responded to different images. I couldn't get the picture of the panicked and grief-stricken families out of my head, the missing-person flyers and the pleas for help. Pat reacted more to the symbolism of the act, to the fact that our country had been attacked. A few days later, Pat gave an interview to NFL Films. "I play football," he said, "and it just seems so—Goddamn, it is unimportant compared to everything that has taken place. I feel guilty even having the damn interview. My grandfather was at Pearl Harbor, a lot of my family has gone and fought in wars, and I really haven't done a damn thing. I think of this—this kind of sounds tacky, but I've always thought about Pearl Harbor, and the people and the boats and the bombs kind of coming down, and what they were going through, their screaming and the passion they exuded and how they lost their lives. I think of stuff like that. I imagine I'll probably have a few other things to think about now, maybe a fireman running up those stairs."

Pat felt like we were living through an important part of history. Life, he saw, was about much more than what was immediately in front of us. He had always loved history and spent a lot of time reading about Winston Churchill, Abraham Lincoln, and other great leaders. Up until that point in our lives, not much had happened in the world that had had the power to shake us up and make us feel called to action. Now Pat did feel called to act. The need to protect and defend was physical to him. Chivalry was embedded in his DNA, evident in the way he'd rush to defend his brothers or his friends, in the way he kindly treated women, in the way he'd internalized stories his mother had told him about the battles of Gettysburg and Bull Run. There are people who don't respond strongly to words like "honor," but Pat did. Those five small letters strung together meant the world to him.

Weeks went by. Pat sustained an ankle injury and focused himself on getting healthy and finishing out the season. We spent a quiet Christmas in Phoenix, just the two of us, the conversation from October tucked away. Even if he'd wanted to enlist September 12, he never would have broken his NFL contract. When the season ended, Pat tried to relax into a few months of off time. He visibly struggled with too much leisure time. Each off-season, he tried to be productive, constantly working to keep his mind and body moving. This off-season was a little different, though; our wedding was only a couple of months away and we spent a lot of time in San Jose, attending to details. All the while, Pat wrestled with the idea of joining the Army. He learned that if he joined the Rangers, he could choose where he wanted to be based, and that Fort Lewis, outside Seattle, was one of those choices. I watched and served as a sounding board as he researched different options, talked to people who had served, and tried to set a plan in place for a path he was instinctively drawn to.

It wasn't really logical for him to join; it was emotional. He felt a larger calling, and never one to shy away from a challenge or let convention get in his way, he ultimately decided this was the path he wanted to take. He felt bad that our wedding was only months away, and told me that if I didn't think it was appropriate to get married right then, he'd understand. I didn't want to postpone the wedding, but I struggled with what this would mean for our lives. I worried about his safety, of course, but at that time I also didn't really think Pat could get hurt or killed. He was smart; he was strong; he'd figure out a way to get through okay. Mainly, I feared missing his company. We'd spent four years apart during college, and I didn't want to go back to that. I loved our quiet little life in Phoenix. I hated when he was gone in the summer at training camp, and long deployments when we'd be away from each other were not what I wanted. We both wanted to start a family as soon as possible, and his enlisting would interfere with that plan. In some of my angry moments, I felt he was being selfish, and told him so. But deep down, I knew it was I who was being selfish.

I hated guns, violence, and war and had always been perplexed by the need for it all. Was fighting just human nature? Was this what we did as people—tried to conquer each other? I didn't completely get it, but still I always admired people who enlisted. I couldn't imagine what it would take for me to do so myself. But that wasn't the point. If Pat had come to me one day and said that he wanted us to join the peace corps, or that he wanted to open a creperie, I would have taken him seriously. I would have said, "Okay, let's talk it through," because that's what our relationship was like.

The only cost would be pushing the pause button for the three years of his enlistment. These years would be only a blip on a long life together. I could imagine us being old, sitting on our rockers, reminiscing: "Remember when you were in the military? That was crazy!" Three years, and then it would be on to the next adventure, maybe one of my choosing.

One Sunday, I was busy Googling away when Pat walked into our home office. He came up behind me, put his hands on the back of the chair, and leaned down to see what I was working on. I had been researching Seattle all morning, getting into the spirit of adventure and excitement a move would bring.

"What are you up to?" he asked.

"Just doing a little research about Seattle," I said. "It's so beautiful there, all the water and trees. It would be a nice change of pace from the desert."

"So what do you think? Could we make it work for a couple of years?" he asked hesitantly.

I knew he was asking much more than if I could handle relocating for a period of time. We had talked through all the pros and cons of his enlistment, but really the items on the lists didn't matter. The decision to join the Army wasn't about all that. It was about Pat's hearing that voice inside, his internal compass pointing him in a different direction, urging him to make a change. It was that part of his character that compelled him to dedicate his life to something more meaningful. It was a part of him, a part I loved. I knew by asking him not to go I would be asking him to be someone he wasn't, and that was something I could never do.

"I think we could really be happy up there," I said.

He kissed the top of my head and left me to my research.

———

When Pat called Kevin to let him know, both of us knew Kevin would join, too. He was playing minor-league baseball but struggling because of a persistent injury, and the military was something he had talked about in the past. He just needed that final push. Truth be told, I worried less about Pat's safety in the military than Kevin's. I knew Pat would never be the same if something happened to Kevin.

Kevin, Pat, and I went to a recruiting office in a strip mall in Mesa. Kevin and I pretended to be a married couple while Pat stood in the background, trying not to attract attention to himself in case anyone recognized him. Army posters dotted the walls, and the recruiter we spoke with was as nondescript as the office he worked in. He took one look at Kevin—young, athletic, clean-cut—and started selling us hard. And though I was completely aware of the job he was trained to do, he must have done it well, because I started feeling more positive about the whole thing. He confirmed that Rangers could choose where they would be based, and that Rangers could serve for three years instead of four. Kevin, Pat, and I went out for lunch afterward to discuss the recruiter's suggestions and what they were going to do. Kevin and Pat were both pretty excited about the Rangers. Soon after, they told the recruiter they were interested, and we started thinking about a move to Fort Lewis.

Basic training would start just six weeks after our wedding. It was official. We were doing this. Kevin, Pat, and I made a pact to keep the news secret until after the wedding. We knew the reaction from friends and family would be mixed, and we wanted to keep the day about the celebration of Pat's and my life together.

Keeping a secret of that magnitude wasn't easy. I was on edge, and though never the type of bride to care much about details like favors and flowers, I cared even less knowing how insignificant all that was compared to what I was hiding. We got a lot of questions the weekend of the wedding about Pat's plans. He was a free agent, and his agent—and many other guests—wanted to know what the story was with his contract. People would ask me, "What's going on? Why is he not signing his contract?" For the first part of the weekend, I was stressed out by all the questions. Then I decided to let it go. It was my wedding day and I was just going to have fun. And I did. Though I probably would have preferred a small wedding, Pat wanted a big party, and so did my parents. The guest list—250 people strong—was the only thing Pat really weighed in on. Well, that and having an open bar.

Our wedding was full of the moments that make for great photography: me in a white dress with an enormous bustle;

Pat and his ten or so groomsmen, decked out in tuxes. There were an elegant staircase, perfectly placed flowers—the whole picture-book fairy tale. Though I didn't relish the moment of walking down the aisle with everyone's eyes on me, it was the most meaningful part of the day to me. With our decision about enlisting, our relationship seemed like it had reached a new level of closeness, of connectedness. Pat and I had already started our new life together, and meeting each other at the altar was a significant symbol of making it official. Without even thinking, Pat and I kissed as soon as I got to the end of the aisle, an act that drew the ire of more-traditional family members, because it went against custom. We didn't care. We were married outdoors by a judge, so we obviously weren't too hung up on custom to begin with.

Overall, the wedding was really more for everyone else than it was for us, and the memories that stayed with me weren't the posed ones. They were my mom's fretting beforehand that Pat wouldn't cut his long hair before the wedding. (Much to her relief, he did.) There was the embarrassment I felt during our first dance, to Ben Harper's "Forever," because everyone was watching us so intently. Then there were Pat's brothers' toasts—Kevin's interrupted by frequent spitting into a wineglass because he was chewing tobacco; Richard's given completely off the cuff. And then there was the fact that Pat wasn't feeling well that day. He'd had food poisoning the day before the wedding, so after the ceremony, we retreated to a private room and he laid his head on my lap for a while.

After the party was over, all our friends decided to go out. Ordinarily, we would have gone with them. Pat probably would have stayed out all night. But we didn't go, because we wanted just to be alone together. Time was starting to feel more precious. We still had our honeymoon to go on, but not a lot of time before he'd be leaving. There were so many changes going on in our life, and they all got wrapped up together. There was a lot of deep meaning to the day, not just a wedding and a party.

So as the party moved to a bar down the street, Pat and I snuck away. Realizing neither of us had eaten all day, we stopped at a little Italian place close to our hotel and ordered a pizza to bring back to our room. I was still in my long white dress, and Pat still in his tuxedo, as we plopped on the bed, the pizza between us, to recap the day. Debriefing was always my favorite part of a fun night out with friends. I loved sitting in bed with Pat, hearing his stories and exchanging bits of gossip. As we had both spent the wedding sober, and most of our guests had not, the moments we'd witnessed were even more amusing than usual. We talked about inconsequential stuff, like who had hooked up with whom and who was really going to have a hard time waking up in the morning. We didn't talk about the biggest piece of gossip—the secret we were keeping. There would be time for that tomorrow.

———

Pat and Kevin shared the enlistment news with their family the very day Pat and I left for our honeymoon in Bora-Bora. We spent a week relaxing in the sunshine, waiting for the drama at home to subside. Bora-Bora is a pretty small island, only eighteen miles in circumference. A little road circles the island, and on a bicycle you can make it around the entire perimeter in just a few hours. On our first day, we woke up, had a lazy breakfast of strong coffee and giant omelets that took up more than half the plate, then walked down to the bike rental store just outside our resort. A variety of colorful beach cruisers lined up outside the storefront, and we each chose one—mine with a cute wicker basket attached to the front—and set out to explore. We rode along the ocean for a while, until Pat motioned for me to pull over to a small fruit stand on the side of the road. We bought two huge slices of watermelon and sat in the grass enjoying the delicious fruit. As we ate, we watched people from the town walk by. Some bought fruit; others just stopped to chat with the owner.

"The locals seem so happy," Pat said. "I mean, they have so little—most of them are walking around with no shoes. I can't imagine there's much work here besides catering to tourists. Yet they all have smiles on their faces and look like they don't have a care in the world."

I'd noticed it, too. "It makes you realize life can be much simpler," I said. "People at home seem so much more unhappy." I tried to push away thoughts of the complicated scenes I felt sure were unfolding in our absence.

"Let's never go back to real life," I said, and lay flat back on the grass. "We could live on an island, right?"

"Definitely," Pat said, and lay back, too. "We could swim every morning."

"And read on the sand all afternoon."

We looked at each other and grinned. Then we didn't say anything at all for a few minutes, but I knew we were thinking the same thing. The truth was, though our lives back home were complicated, we were excited for the future. Pat was looking forward to the military; he wouldn't have enlisted if he'd felt otherwise. And I was excited about being married and moving together to a new place, to start our new adventure.

When we returned to real life, relaxed and tanned, we heard at once from our families. Both Pat's family and mine had determined they weren't going to let the enlistment decision go without a fight. They arranged an intervention of sorts, calling us all together to talk it out. Always willing to let people speak their minds, Pat welcomed the discussion, and we headed back to San Jose for the family meeting. I understood their panic. Though

Pat and I had worked out this decision over months, our families had had only a week to digest it all. Dannie was pretty emotional, as was my mom. My dad tried to make a logical case for Pat's not enlisting while Christine sat quietly in the background and Alex, being Alex, took on the role of mediator. Appeals were made to me to stop Pat, which only made me feel more aligned with Kevin and Pat. We weren't kids anymore, but since we were still young and had gotten together young, I think we still seemed childlike to our parents. I understood their need to change our minds, but there was no turning back.

The decision was made. This was our life, and this was what we wanted to do with it. Pat, Kevin, and I were joined in a higher purpose, setting forward on an adventure that we knew would be difficult, but that would ultimately nourish our lives and help us grow.

CHAPTER FIVE

Two months after our wedding, Pat and Kevin left for basic training in Georgia. They'd be there for three months, and I wasn't sure how often I would be able to talk to Pat. Knowing the separation would be difficult, Pat wrote me a note before he left.

July 8, 2002

Marie,
I know this isn't the direction you saw us moving...
I know this isn't the life you dream to live...
I know at times this path will be rough...
And, I know at times you'll feel alone.
However...

I know you are strong...
I know this path has an end...
I know someday you'll have the life you dream...
And, I know this direction will ultimately lead to happiness.
However, despite what I know...
Regardless of our direction, dreams, or path...
I know we have each other and that I love you...
And that's all I need to know.

Pat

Pat's words helped, but I think he needed them as much as I did. When he was finally able to call me from basic training, he couldn't even speak because he was so choked up. I started chatting, filling the silence with the mundane details of my day—that I'd found renters for our place in Arizona, that I'd gotten everything packed up—anything to help him calm down and not have to focus on how miserable he was. I hated hearing him upset but wasn't too surprised. By then, I was used to the stabilizing role I played in his life, and I knew that it was hard for him to be away.

When we hung up, I hardened my resolve to take good care of the details of our lives. It had fallen to me to find us a home near Fort Lewis. The first place I looked at when I got to Washington was what became our little cottage perched up on a hill overlooking the narrows.

The house had been built in the 1920s and had up until recently served as a home for the owner's mother. I admired its good bones, polished wood floors, and big front windows. The flowered wallpaper made it feel a bit like a granny's house, but after the owner agreed to let me paint and make a few changes, I knew it would be perfect. I put down a deposit, signed the lease, and made plans to return in a month. My mom graciously agreed to return with me and helped me with the cleaning, painting, decorating, and unpacking of all our wedding gifts. The cottage's scenic setting invited contemplation, and its cozy feel invited guests. It was perfect.

When he finally saw it, Pat loved it. His mom's house had a cottagey feel, too, and I think he loved the similarity. He smiled widely the first time he saw it. He walked from room to room, exploring the house's nooks and crannies, and I felt rewarded for all the hard work. The house became a safe haven for him from the difficulties of military life.

Pat's early months in the military were hard for him. He was a leader and an independent thinker, an aberration in the rank-and-file military system. Yet after a lifetime of speaking his mind, he was not invited to do so. When he and Kevin weren't overseas, Pat would come home from a day at Fort Lewis and tell me with frustration that he'd mowed lawns all day. He had a hard time when authority was held by someone he didn't respect. "I'm too old for this shit," he'd say. "I can drop to the ground and give them fifty push-ups, but I don't want to, because it's stupid." He'd think, *Here this horrific thing happened on 9/11, and I have something to contribute, and I'm mowing lawns.* His intelligence and life experience weren't valued in the military structure and this frustrated him. During basic training, he felt like he'd gone from a full-on adult who had a home and responsibilities, who was 100 percent in control of his life, to someone who had to ask to go to the bathroom. And make no mistake about it: From the time he was a little kid, Pat was always the guy in control. He wondered if he could have contributed to the cause in another way. Given his stature in Arizona, running for office wouldn't have been outside the realm of possibility. Of course, Pat was aware from the get-go that he'd struggle with this aspect of the military, but you can never really prepare for a loss of independence of that magnitude.

For the most part, I was sympathetic and tried to do what I could to make his home life easy, given what he was going through. But I had limits. Pat had to take a physical fitness test before he could go to Ranger school. The guy who was counting his sit-ups didn't like him and claimed a few of Pat's sit-ups weren't done correctly. As a result, Pat didn't pass. He called me at work right after it happened, and he was practically having a nervous breakdown because of the lack of control he had over the situation. He moped for days afterward, and I got frustrated. "I never see you," I told him. "And now you're home, and yet you're acting like an ass. You're wasting this precious time that we have together being grumpy about sit-ups." He heard me, got over it, and passed the test the next time around. This was one of the few arguments we got in during that period.

Throughout our relationship, we never fought about major issues, just stupid stuff. Sometimes I would be mad about something, and Pat wouldn't even argue. He'd just say, "What's going on? You're being a lunatic," and it would stop there. We were both really good about realizing when we were in the wrong, and coming around to reason. But once Pat enlisted, there wasn't time for even our low-key brand of argument. Little stuff like his sloppy bathroom habits didn't bother me at all; our time together was too precious to debate things like toilet seat lids and toothpaste caps.

———

Pat and Kevin were gone a lot during the time we lived in Washington. They had boot camp and Ranger school, and altogether, they were deployed overseas twice: the first time to Iraq, the second to Afghanistan.

The Iraq deployment was unexpected, and when it came on, it came on fast. In what seemed like only minutes after we'd settled in Washington, the Bush administration turned their sights on the country, and a conflict was imminent. Pat's squadron started training in full-on chemical warfare jumpsuits and got anthrax vaccinations, and the danger of military service became very, very real and very, very scary. He and Kevin left for Baghdad or god-knows-where; I wasn't told. To make matters worse, neither Pat nor I agreed with the Iraq War. With nearly every other world leader against the invasion, it didn't seem like a wise thing to do. We felt it was illegal and unjust. "I'll do my job," Pat told me one night before he left, when we were discussing the war. "But I don't think our role there is virtuous at all."

When you sign up for the military, you understand that you will be following someone's orders, whether you agree or not, and whether you respect the orders or not. Pat understood and accepted that basic principle going in. But that didn't mean that training in a Hazmat suit for a war he didn't believe in was easy, or that silencing his thoughts on the issue was a small matter. He had been opinionated from the moment I'd met him. In fact, he'd often take a stance that he didn't even really believe to get a rise out of someone and ensure a lively debate on an issue. His close family and friends would anticipate and relish the conversations on subjects ranging from how to make the perfect cup of coffee to what California should do about immigration. I was probably the only exception. When Pat took an extreme stand on an issue with me, I'd just smile and say, "I'm not going to argue with you about that—you don't even believe it. I don't want to spend the energy having a debate with you about something you don't even believe in." But we did talk at length about President Bush, the Iraq War, and what the US role should be. Pat struggled with the ethical issues presented to him, and his feelings on the matter certainly dampened his enthusiasm about service and made our sacrifices feel all the more acute. But ultimately, he'd made a commitment and felt it wasn't right to back out of a commitment just because it turned out differently than he'd anticipated.

Once, after Pat and Kevin had left, I was driving home, and I passed an antiwar protest outside Fort Lewis. I was struck by a protestor who identified herself as the mother of a soldier. Could I stand with her? I wanted to, and I thought about it a lot. I fully felt you could support the troops and yet not the military actions. Plus the decisions made in Washington now affected me in a very real, personal way, and far from feeling I needed to be loyal, I felt I needed to be even more involved in and outspoken about what those decisions were. I needed to remind removed decision makers that there were flesh-and-blood individuals' lives at stake. But at this point in time, the antiwar platform was raw, shaky ground to stand on. Pat was already treated differently from other servicemen because of his NFL background, and didn't welcome the attention. I didn't want to make it worse for him. I drove past and went home.

When Pat was away, I worried constantly. I knew I shouldn't watch the news, but I was obsessed with it and couldn't turn it off. CNN would report that a helicopter had gone down, and I'd panic. I had no idea where Pat and Kevin were. The soft sound of a car passing the house in the middle of the night would wake me; my heart would pound as I'd wait for it to stop in our driveway, for the footsteps on the porch, and for the knock at the door that would change my life.

I didn't share any of my distress with Pat. I knew that the more stable I was emotionally, the easier it was for him to do his job and focus. A lot of pressure falls on the shoulders of military families in this way. I put a lot of energy into the show of functioning. I wanted to be sure that when I heard from Pat and he asked me what I'd been up to, I'd be able to tell him about the museums I'd visited, the books I'd read, the friends I'd made. And I did do all these things. It was during this time that I first learned how to live alone. I learned how to take care of the bills on time; I learned how to change a flat tire. I had essentially moved to Washington by myself, found a job by myself, and made friends by myself. The effort was not lost on Pat, who wrote in a letter from Iraq:

It's hard to think about how bad this situation really is sometimes. I hate being away from you, I hate the fact that you're growing into a life so far removed from me. Don't mistake me, I'm incredibly proud and impressed with everything you've done these past months. Your attitude, good humor and general greatness have made this awful experience bearable. I love us, our family, and feel somehow I'm just missing out. What the fuck kind of marriage involves my absence for months at a time? This is truly terrible and I think I may actually be a bad person for putting you through this. It's funny because at the time I felt that any absence would be tolerable due to the "cause" or whatever concept I deluded myself into believing I was standing for. I'm a fool. How I managed to find a way out of our perfect existence is incredible. I know I've rambled like this countless times saying the same shit, so I'll go ahead and stop. I figured you might actually like to see how miserable I am without you. Of course you're not happy that I'm miserable, however there is that small satisfaction in knowing I need you. Well that's why I whined, it was all for you. Selfless as always...

Letters like this were like dips in my emotional roller coaster. I'd go weeks without hearing from Pat, then would receive several letters in one group only a couple of days before he got home. I felt terrible about Pat's guilt, and yet part of me found gratification in his recognition of my sacrifice. I was putting a lot of effort into making things seem okay, and I was grateful that he knew that. Unlike when I'd made sacrifices for his football career, this time he seemed to really grasp his work's toll on me and understand that the things that I needed to be happy and fulfilled weren't material at all, but were entirely wrapped up in being near him. But my feelings of gratification quickly led to feelings of guilt. On top of all the other stresses he had, I didn't want him to worry about me. I did my best to shake the whole mess of emotions off, to regroup, and just when I had, another letter from Pat would arrive.

I'm sitting in my little fighting position while half my squad leaves for a recon. mission. I'm tired, pretty hungry and incredibly filthy. My surroundings are trees, green, swamp, hills and heavy rucksacks, yet my mind is far from any of this. My mind is on you and the visualization of our children. What will they be like? Who will they look like? Will they be a combination of the two of us or take shape in either of our personalities at all? Perhaps one will look and act just like you while the others me or vice versa. Perhaps they'll look like your mom or have my grandfather's demeanor, Kevin's nose or Paul's figure. Maybe we'll have small skinny daughters built lean like our fathers and short legged sons like our moms. I can't wait to pick out those traits as I stare into their faces. I can't wait to watch them take shape and grow from aspects of others' to a whole unique unto itself. I can't wait to see how excited my mom will look when I tell her you're pregnant. I can't wait to sit in Alex and Christine's living room laughing about all the ridiculous nonsense our kids are up to. I can't wait to be proud of our daughter when she stars as "Happy Toad" in the school play. I imagine watching Kevin teach our son to hit a baseball, Paul showing him plans for his next big real estate deal, Alex teaching him the stars and of being a good person and man through stories about his grandpa....I can't wait to watch you and Christine blow all our money on shopping trips with our spoiled daughters. I look forward to the day your Dad takes our son to a Giants game, or Richard bringing the kids down to show them Hollywood for the weekend....I see us driving down the road with the kids laughing at me for something stupid I said from the back of our new Volvo. I look forward to watching you breastfeed the little guy....I can't wait to see the look in your eyes after your first labor. Everything we've done in the past will pale in comparison to the adventure of the family we will soon have. So much to be excited about....

Refolding the letter, I was thrown into a negative tailspin, with a power and force I submitted to. Pat was trying to be strong, and hopeful, but his letter just made me regret all the things we were missing out on *now*. My friends all called with news of their pregnancies, or the trips they were taking with their husbands, and I'd feel sorry for myself that I couldn't call them with the same news. I was constantly fighting my natural inclination to stay home and wallow. *Go out, Marie,* I'd tell myself. *Go meet people so you have something to write to Pat about; go somewhere to snap yourself out of feeling sorry for yourself.* But after this letter, I needed a break from finding something positive in the situation and let myself give in to being depressed. There were days when I wouldn't leave the house, but I'd never let Pat know. With all he was going through, it didn't seem fair to put that on him, too.

As strong as each of us tried to be for the other, stress has a way of spilling over when it's been contained for too long. A couple of days before Pat's last deployment, to Afghanistan, he went to the basement to get his stuff together, and I followed him. Our quaint cottage was old and had paper-thin walls, so there was little opportunity for private conversation, and I'd been stewing for hours. Pat's family was in town, camped out in our living room. They had wanted to see him and Kevin before their deployment, and though they'd been there several days already, they had just decided to extend their trip a few days. While I loved Pat's family and enjoyed having them around, time alone together had become too precious. Pat was the oldest brother, the first married, so I was also struggling with a tension most new couples experience: establishing that a new family unit had been borne out of those wedding vows. But mostly, I was anxious about this deployment—more so than the last one—because now I knew what lay ahead: the months of constant worry and a silent house. I yearned to have Pat all to myself for a day. I would have even taken a couple of hours. When I walked into the basement, Pat could tell instantly that something was wrong. Tears started spilling down my cheeks, and I was so upset I could barely get the words out.

"Why can't they all go home?" I cried. "It's been several days already!"

Just two minutes earlier, I'd seemed fine, so Pat looked at me like I'd lost my mind. In some ways, I had. He started to get defensive and argue with me, but then he stopped. He could see my stress and the emotional toll this experience was taking. I was acting clingy and needy, which was in sharp contrast to the independent, stoic nature I'd developed since this adventure had begun. He put his arms around me, realizing that was all I really needed. We sat like that for a while, just a few silent moments, on the cold steps of the basement, a load of laundry at our feet.

———

The hole left when Pat died took on various forms. He'd been gone for a year, and still I missed the physical being of him, his strong gentle touch and the warmth of his body in bed. I missed his friendship. For over ten years of my life, whenever something would happen, whether it was an unpleasant encounter with a grocery clerk or a major current event, it was Pat who I would think of first and want to call. I trusted his instincts and ability to see the world. I trusted his ability to weigh the pros and cons of a situation. It wasn't until he was gone that I realized that many people never have this, and learned how lonely the world can be when navigated alone.

Parts of my brain shut down entirely. Memories became frozen, inaccessible. I panicked at first, though I logically understood there was an inverse relationship between stress and memory. Your brain makes you handle only what you can handle. But I desperately needed to recall things like which eye had the fleck of gold near the pupil, what we had eaten the last time we'd had dinner together, what the warmth of his skin through a thin white T-shirt felt like. I needed to remember that his broken pinky stuck out when he drank coffee, that too much carbonation bothered his stomach. The way his tongue pushed against his teeth when he pronounced certain words, and the way he ordered his lattes extra, extra hot, because adding the second "extra" let them know he was serious. I needed the comfort of these memories, but the more I tried to remember, the less I was able to recall, the more panicked I became, and the vicious cycle began anew.

Though still young, I became obsessed with my own

mortality and—worse yet—with the idea that an accident would leave me incapacitated and dependent on others. What would I do? There was no one around to make me soup if I got sick or take me to the doctor if I needed to go. I knew these thoughts were ridiculous but suddenly, they didn't seem that way. The worst thing I could ever imagine had happened; it had come true. At first I thought, *Well, there you go. This terrible thing has happened to me, so that's my allotment in life—from here on out, no more bad will come.* But then I realized, no, that's not the way it works. Sometimes people face enormous loss and adversity while others get through life unscathed. I lay awake at night paralyzed by the fear of all the other awful things that potentially lay ahead. Things just happen. Randomly and awfully, they just happen. I wished that I felt otherwise, that I was a religious person who believed that everything happens for a reason. I'd even tried to tap into a spiritual answer and had sat on the porch the night after Pat died, asking for some sort of sign or feeling that there was a heaven and that I'd see him again. But I'd felt nothing. I didn't feel that he was in a better place, that this was all part of god's plan, or that everything happened for a reason. I simply felt nothing.

I second-guessed everything. One night after walking for hours, I came home with no idea of what to do next. Eat? Watch TV? Even small decisions, like how to fill the time, I couldn't make on my own. I walked into the bedroom, flipped on the light, and fell back on the bed. On the nightstand sat a few how-to-grieve books, sent by practical people, with tips like finding a new hobby or changing your routine. After reading one particularly unhelpful passage, suggesting if you always ate dinner together at six p.m. in the dining room, try eating at five p.m. in the kitchen, I threw the book across the room. It hit the wall with a thump, landing with its pages splayed out on the floor. I didn't need a new hobby or a change in dinner schedule; I needed real help. I needed to figure out a way to live again, as Pat had asked me to, but the wisdom of how to do this eluded me.

Lying faceup, staring at the ceiling, I finally decided I should go get something to eat. I couldn't remember the last time I'd had anything more substantial than coffee. Some days I forced myself to eat, but just enough so that I wouldn't pass out and call attention to my shrinking self. I welcomed that empty feeling in my belly. I felt more right as a hollow shell.

I twisted to get up and something caught my eye. A book had fallen off the nightstand and lay wedged between the bed and wall. I pulled it out and saw it was Pat's dog-eared copy of Ralph Waldo Emerson's *Self-Reliance*. Along with a handful of novels, he had taken this slim book of essays to Iraq. It had touched his soul, and when he returned, he continued to read and reread its contents. One quiet evening, he was lying on the couch reading while I folded laundry in the bedroom. He became excited by what he was reading, and wanting to share, he burst in, quoting passages, as I folded T-shirts.

His enthusiasm when he found something he loved had been contagious, and tears welled up in my eyes as I held his book and pictured the joy on his face that evening. I flipped through the pages and saw his carefully underlined passages.

"Nothing can bring you peace but yourself." It was like he was speaking to me, lighting the darkness with the marks of his pen and the poetic words of Emerson. A smile began to form, but the pulling of the expression on my face felt strange and stopped me halfway.

I eagerly scanned the book, underlined passages leaping out at me. "Be not the slave to your own past. Plunge into the sublime seas, dive deep and swim far, so you shall come back with self-respect, with new power, with an advanced experience that shall explain and overlook the old."

After that night, the little book of essays rarely left my side. I would turn to it in my darkest times to find insight, or just to see Pat's pen drawn across the page. The book allowed me somehow to get inside his head and find a way out of the heaviness that consumed my days and nights.

Slowly, a shift began. I started to see a small glimmer of faith—not in the mystical, but in myself. I started to see that while I couldn't control what happened in life, I could control my reaction to it. I saw two roads ahead of me: one of self-pity and destruction, and the other less certain, but more open and light. Maybe I could learn to live. When a friend called not long afterward to see if I wanted to go on a last-minute trip to Hawaii, my immediate reaction was to put up walls. The trip was too soon; the flight was going to be too expensive; I had to work. But I couldn't help noticing a strange feeling rise to the top of the list. I wanted to go. I wanted to feel the sand in my toes, lounge in the sun, swim in the salty ocean. *Two roads, Marie,* I thought. *Let's not take the self-pity road for just a little while.* I got off the phone, searched online, and booked my ticket.

The comfort and calm I'd found in Emerson's words led me to seek out other great thinkers for insight. To the endless hours of aimless walking that occupied my weekends, I added hours in the bookstore searching for books I would take home by the armful. I read volumes from Thoreau, Jean-Paul Sartre, Nietzsche, Kierkegaard, and Viktor Frankl, absorbing the parts that spoke to me, dismissing the rest, and piecing together my own framework to build from. It wasn't only philosophy that gave me comfort, but also stories of tragedy and triumph over adversity. These dark tales seemed more true to my own life than the stories of people I encountered every day. I was looking for connection in the similar arc of one human life to another, a clue for how to get through, or just comfort in knowing I was not alone in my suffering.

One of the books I found solace in was Joan Didion's

The Year of Magical Thinking, about the year her husband suddenly died and her daughter became critically ill. With elegance and artistry, she captured the ups, downs, and sideways moves that characterize those first twelve months of loss. *But what happens then?* I wondered as I finished it. For Pat had been gone more than a year, and a time had come that was as scary as any before it. It was time for me to make decisions bigger than how to fill a free hour.

Namely, the end of Kevin's enlistment was in sight, and I needed to decide whether to stay in Washington or leave. And if the answer was leave, where would I go? Though there were many things I loved about the Seattle area, I couldn't imagine staying. I had family and roots in San Jose, friends in Arizona, but neither felt right. Because of an instinct that I'd first had in high school, while fantasizing about faraway schools, and that had peeped up again after college graduation, New York City felt right. "Be not the slave to your own past." I had always wanted to live in New York, and it was different from anything I'd ever known. My defenses were kicking in; my natural survival mode was taking over and taking care of everything. New York was many miles away from anyone I knew, and I could heal in my own way— no intrusions, no dropping by, no inquisitive eyes wondering *How's Marie today?* Just me and a city full of strangers. I could wander the streets for hours and see hundreds of people but no one would know my past or care. It was just what I needed. I arranged to transfer to the New York office of my company, because I knew I'd need an anchor in New York.

With the biggest decision made, I made another: to get the most out of my last few months in Washington. I hadn't taken a road trip since Pat had died, and I wanted to get out on the open highway again and really see the Northwest. I read an article in a magazine about kitesurfers on Hood River in Oregon, a mere three-and-a-half-hour drive away. Why not go check it out for myself? With Kevin out of town for the weekend, unfilled hours stretching ahead of me, and weather that was starting to warm, it made good sense.

Traveling solo was a new experience. There was no one to help navigate while I drove, and often I had to pull over to look at the map. But driving along with the windows down made me feel freer than I had in the confinement of the house. I loved our little house, but I was starting to feel the walls caving in; the once comfortable cocoon was beginning to feel suffocating. On the open highway, I already felt better and was applauding myself for the decision to get out. As the pine trees and billboards whizzed by and southern Washington gave way to northern Oregon, I was reminded how satisfying it was to log miles, to cover ground.

It took longer than it should have, but I got where I wanted to go. I pulled over in the little town and bought a cup of coffee from a shop that sold muffins and surf gear alongside espresso. Then I found a spot at the area's central park to watch the kitesurfers do their thing. The wind whipped my hair around my face, and I tucked it back behind my ears so I could see the large colorful kites dotting the skyline, the snowcapped peak of Mount Hood visible behind them. The riders stood up on small surfboards, maneuvering the kites as they propelled the riders along the waves. I watched for a few minutes, fascinated by the skill of the riders, then thought, *Now what?* If Pat had been there, he would have tried it out, and I would have cheered, snapped photos, and laughed at him from shore. We would have listened to music during the entire drive, instead of the silence I now preferred. Maybe we would have had dinner in the little town; maybe we would have spent the night at one of the small inns or bed-and-breakfasts dotting the shoreline. But at least I was there. At least I'd gotten there. I finished what was left of my coffee, and just thirty minutes after arriving, I got back in the car for the long drive home.

PART 2: 2005–2007

The present in New York is so powerful that the past is lost.

—John Jay Chapman

CHAPTER SIX

On a lazy Saturday afternoon after I arrived in New York, I made my way through the stalls of the Union Square farmer's market to Fifth Avenue. I was just window-shopping, but something caught my eye and I ducked into the store to take a closer look. The front table was piled with cashmere sweaters in the most beautiful colors I'd ever seen—bright peacock blue, purple, lemon yellow. I ran my hand across the soft piles, landing on a cardigan that was a shade somewhere between bubble gum and hot pink. I'm strictly a black, white, brown, navy kind of girl. I don't wear color—never have—and certainly not pink, but I picked it up and walked over to the mirror. I slipped it over my T-shirt, and suddenly my cheeks seemed rosier. For an instant, I glimpsed the younger, more carefree version of myself I had almost forgotten. Pink or not, I had to have it.

The vibrancy of the city was rubbing off on me, just as I knew it would. I hadn't come for the Carrie Bradshaw experience; I had come for an energy transfusion in the deep privacy of the anonymous city. And it seemed to be working. In Washington I had walked my pain through the sleepy, winding roads above the narrows; here I walked it through the city's chaotic flow, but the flow alone made me feel more alive. One of my favorite writers, Pico Iyer, wrote that "our highest moments come when we are not stationary," and I hoped that if I just kept moving, internal transition would follow my external one.

As I walked the streets of New York, there could be no silence. Music found me; color leapt out from the billboards and storefronts. It was a relief to look with open eyes at nature blooming all around me—not only the trees and flower boxes but the young, bright faces of couples, with their snippets of conversation, as they passed.

With its busy sidewalks, great museums, and expansive park, I felt the beauty and energy of the city seeping in and making me smile, despite everything, as I walked. I was looking for an express train out of grief, and New York was home to the fastest track in the world. I knew the news surrounding my life would be forgotten soon enough by the rest of the country, but it was already ancient history in New York, which metabolizes news as fast as the ever-bursting printing presses can fill the newsstands with fresh horrors.

In New York, I could try on a different persona with every new encounter. One day I went to get a haircut at a place down the street from my apartment. My hairdresser was an edgy, tattooed young girl named Claire, with an auburn bob and bluntly cut bangs. She ran her fingers through my long blonde hair, examining the ends and the handiwork of my previous stylist, and we talked for a minute about the cut I wanted. After she shampooed and combed my hair out, the requisite small talk began.

"So do you work in the city?"

"Yes," I said, and decided to be vague without being impolite. "I work in Midtown."

"Cool," she said, and went back to snipping my dead ends. The silence felt a little awkward, so I made a point of turning the page of my magazine so she would think I was engrossed rather than ignoring her. When she saw me flip the page, she must have noticed my wedding ring.

"How about your husband?" she asked, trying again. "What's he do?"

"Oh," I said, looking up and meeting her eyes in the mirror for a second, "um, he works in high tech."

"Cool. You guys are new to the city?"

"We just moved here from Washington State." I went on about how we had moved a month earlier for a job opportunity, and how we both loved the energy of New York City. I wove an elaborate story of half-truths and lies, unable to stop myself, wanting so badly for the life I was telling her about to be my reality. While I liked my haircut, I realized when I left that I couldn't go back to see Claire. What if I didn't remember all my lies correctly? I chastised myself on the walk home, feeling that somehow, because of the charade, I wasn't being true to Pat. But then I remembered he used to tell harmless lies like that, too. In fact, the tech field had become sort of an inside joke with us. Since we were from Silicon Valley, half the people we knew worked in the amorphous "tech" industry. When Pat first started playing football, he would sometimes tell people he did, too, because he didn't want to look like a braggart. Since tech is massive, complicated, and, frankly, a bit boring to those who don't work in it, usually polite inquisitors didn't bother to follow up. Pat would have laughed at my white lie. If anyone would understand my aversion to being labeled "widow," it would be him. The widow label was not true to who I was. Kevin in particular hated it, assuring me on occasion that I wasn't some poisonous black spider.

The only person in New York who knew my whole story was my new boss, Maura. When I'd first moved, I had transferred to the New York office of my Seattle company, but without the camaraderie I'd felt with the Seattle group, the job itself seemed pointless. So I accepted a job with Maura at ESPN. Maura was a producer, and I was her right-hand woman. I'd met her when Pat was alive, as she'd wanted to do a story on him for the network. He'd declined, but Maura kept in touch and I'd become friends with her in the time that followed. I felt a great deal of affection for her. Ten years older than me, she was blonde and rail-thin, smoked like a chimney, and took her toy terrier, Maggie, everywhere with her. Her style was blunt, a bit rough around the edges, but she was also very real. An incredibly intense businesswoman, she was married only to her job. While my role—which consisted largely of catering to celebrities and project-managing events—didn't hold a great deal of appeal to me in and of itself, it swept me up and filled my days with traveling, soothing people's egos, extinguishing fires, and generally trying to keep pace with Maura's high-energy train. There was never silence at work, never time to think. It was ideal.

One day after finishing up some plans for our next event, I plopped down on the small couch in Maura's office. She was sitting behind her desk, Maggie perched on her lap, and she looked at me head-on and said, "I get it now, Marie."

I smiled quizzically. Maura would often start conversations this way. I wouldn't know where she was going, but I would try to be ready for whatever she was going to throw at me.

"I was thinking last night," she continued, "about how

I would feel if I lost this job. I wouldn't even know who I was. And I get it. I get how you feel."

Maura's equating Pat's death with the loss of a job didn't strike me as at all insensitive. I knew how much her job meant to her, and understood the spirit of her comment. She was trying to relate and empathize with me, and in many ways, she was right. Not only had I lost Pat, I'd lost the identity of who I'd been as Pat's wife. The identity piece of my grief was a struggle I was starting to recognize in other people—friends who'd lost jobs or broken up with a partner, or even new moms, like my sister, who'd left one life for a foreign one.

While I had identified myself strongly with my relationship with Pat, his identity was not wrapped around it. It wasn't that he didn't care about the relationship as much as I did; he just didn't see identity that way. He wasn't husband, son, student, football player, soldier. He was all those things, of course, but none of those things. That was part of the reason he wouldn't talk to the press after he decided to leave the NFL for the military. He knew the press would make him into a symbol, and he didn't want that when the truth was much more nuanced, when people are much more nuanced. It was one of the reasons he took to studying in college. Because he was a college football player—and a good one—people wanted to identify him as "jock," but he wanted none of that. So while he hadn't been much of a student in high school, in college he delighted in defying people's expectations, earning great grades and graduating early.

I tried to emulate the way Pat saw identity, but sometimes the world seems to offer only boxes—like paperwork asking me to bubble in my marital status, or a hairdresser innocently asking about my husband's job. One evening, the simple act of getting dressed to go out brought up all kinds of identity issues. I put on my fourth shirt of the hour, but after looking in the mirror, I grimaced and pulled it off. I was twenty-nine, not fifty-nine, but felt like my pre-widow standbys of skinny jeans and a slinky top wouldn't be appropriate. I didn't want to wear anything too exposed or revealing, and I didn't want to draw any male attention. Even talking flirtatiously with another guy—let alone dating—was definitely out of the question.

I was supposed to meet up with Kelly, a friend of a Seattle friend of mine. The Seattle friend, Michelle, had connected us soon after I'd moved to New York. Michelle said Kelly was great and had a cool group of girlfriends that I should get to know. Our meeting was a big deal for me, as I always had to gear myself up for social situations and the energy they required. I glanced at the clock and saw I was already running late. I pulled on a black long-sleeved shirt from the pile on my bed, dabbed on a little lip gloss, and ran out the door. I texted Kelly from the cab to let her know I was running late but would be there shortly. I lied, telling her I was stuck in traffic. The cab pulled up at the downtown restaurant and I saw two girls standing out front, stylishly dressed in short skirts, tights, and knee-high riding boots. I immediately felt old and frumpy. This was a bad idea. I wasn't even inside yet and already was feeling shaky and insecure. *Get it together*, I told myself. I brushed it off, paid the driver, and went inside, where I quickly found Kelly and her crew squished around a table upstairs. Kelly introduced me to everyone, and I tried to relax.

Michelle had been right: They were all great girls. They were young and ambitious, working mostly creative jobs in marketing, publicity, and television. This was what I had come for; this was what I had imagined life would be like in New York. I would move here and be able to join the ranks of young women like this, women who were both working and playing hard and enjoying life. All my friends from home were married by twenty-seven, and a large number of them already had kids. Among my childhood friends, I stood out as a tragic figure, or at least I thought I did. In New York, women wouldn't necessarily be married at twenty-two, or even thirty-two or forty-two. They wouldn't talk about husbands and kids all the time, but about politics, books, and current events. They would live independently, travel, work, and drink and eat well.

The women around me proved I had imagined it correctly. They talked about problems at work, and I tried to commiserate. This wasn't so bad, I thought. Why had

I been so nervous about this? As the evening wore on, though, the conversation turned to troubles with men. "He sent a nice text after our dinner, then went AWOL," said the woman on my left, perplexed. "What do you think that means?" As the other women weighed in with their analysis, I stayed silent. Everyone had a story to tell about a guy who fell off the face of the earth and stopped communication after several seemingly good dates. I had nothing to add. I hadn't dated in over ten years, and things had been much different back then. Somehow, I didn't think the game of capture the flag was similar to any recent experiences these women might have had. The longer I listened to them compare stories of heartache, the more I withdrew.

I should have told the taxi to keep going; I wasn't ready for this, not even close. How could I have a normal conversation with this nice, engaging group when I'd spent the day doing something so foreign to their world? For while they had spent their afternoon navigating office politics and analyzing text messages, I'd spent my afternoon trying to keep Pat's autopsy photos off the Internet.

———

My relationship with the military over the past several years had gotten complex, to say the least. It started just a few days after Pat died, when members of the Casualty Assistance team came to the cottage. They had piles of paperwork for me to fill out and I just blindly signed page after page, as long as they kept feeding me information about when Pat would be flown out of Afghanistan and returned home. One member of the team was going through a list of things that were going to happen, but I barely paid attention until I heard "...and there's going to be his military funeral."

"Wait a minute," I said. "That's not right. That's not what he wanted."

"No," the casualty guy said, correcting me, "it is; it's the way it's done."

A couple of months before Pat was deployed to Afghanistan, he'd brought home all this paperwork he'd had to sign indicating his wishes in case he was killed. He wasn't supposed to photocopy it, but he did, and he gave it to me. "I just have a feeling," he'd said. "I just have a feeling they might try to go against what I've signed, so you should hold on to these." I'd taken them and filed them away in the bedroom; then we'd gone back to eating dinner or doing whatever we'd been doing—because when you are a military family, you can't function if you dwell too much on things like why those forms might be needed.

As the Casualty Assistance Officer stood before me, I remembered that conversation and retrieved the paperwork. "Clearly," I said, shoving it in front of him, "you can see that a military funeral is *not* what he wanted." I was furious. "So why don't you leave?" He looked surprised. No doubt he didn't expect me to have any sort of documentation. He did as I asked and left.

Well over a year had passed since then, and my interaction with the military had only increased as Pat's family and I continued to seek resolution about how Pat had died and why we hadn't been told the truth from the beginning. Dannie in particular was persistent, and spent hours meticulously combing through investigations to make some sense of what had happened. She made lists; she asked questions; she made it clear that she would not rest until the whole story was out. I marveled at my mother-in-law's strength. She seemed to have never-ending reserves of fearlessness and determination. If it hadn't been for her, I don't know how far we would have taken a search for the truth.

All we'd learned for certain was that an ill-advised and much-contested decision to split Pat's platoon led to a confusing firefight in a canyon, where a Humvee of Rangers led by Greg Baker fired on Pat and several others in his group, killing an Afghan military forces soldier and Pat. While this was the basic story, there were a lot of inconsistencies, and we couldn't get answers to key questions, such as why no one saw the smoke flare Pat threw out—which he had on hand expressly to identify himself as a "friendly"—why rules of engagement weren't followed, and why his uniform and protective vest were burned, when they provided evidence as to how he had been killed.

Dannie and I were in near-constant contact, as the Freedom of Information Act required me—as Pat's next of kin—to submit excessive amounts of paperwork to get Pat's records released. After what seemed a ridiculous series of steps, I received his autopsy report.

I read through the document once, not understanding all the medical terminology but knowing the final outcome. *CAUSE OF DEATH: Gunshot Wounds to the Head.* Certain details seemed off: His height was wrong; they noted a gold-colored wedding ring, whereas his ring was platinum; a 3¾ x 3½-inch area on his left upper chest suggested there'd been an attempt at defibrillation, but why would anyone have tried to resuscitate him when, according to what we'd been told, it was gruesomely clear he was gone? I began to wonder if they'd given us the wrong autopsy. Dannie had received the report as well and had the same funny feeling. She called me at work, and in hushed tones we discussed that something was not right. Why weren't we being given accurate information and straight answers? I did not want to have this conversation at work, but it never would have occurred to me not to pick up the phone when Dannie was on the other end of the line.

When Pat and Kevin had enlisted, we had felt unified as a family but also felt we were part of a much bigger, military family. We were all in this together. That's why our treatment after his death felt like such a betrayal. And the thing is once you've been lied to, you start to think no one's telling the truth. Conspiracy theories about Pat's death had started to circulate almost from the beginning—some from credible newspapers. One journalist claimed to have gotten access to top secret forensic evidence that proved Pat had been shot in the head at close range—from not more than thirty feet away. If that was the case, no mistaken-identity claim would hold. Pat was high profile, Pat was outspoken, and Pat was a critic of the Iraq War—a critic who would soon be out of the military. Was it possible that all the fog and lies and confusion were about something much more sinister than fratricide? While the frame of mind I was in caused me to consider that possibility, I really didn't think Pat's death was a murder. If the government had wanted Pat out of the way, there were surely cleaner ways to do it than the confusing firefight that had transpired.

The most extreme conspiracy theorists faded away, and it became clear to me that gross negligence was behind the accident. Soldiers are supposed to identify their target before firing, and among other horrible mistakes, that hadn't happened. One soldier involved even admitted that he hadn't identified his target because he wanted to stay in the firefight. It also became clear that if the military hadn't felt it impossible to cover up, we never would have learned that Pat's death was a fratricide. The war was going badly when he died—very badly. And whether he'd wanted to or not, Pat had been the military's highest-profile enlistee. The motivation was not hard to understand: Surely if the blunders and misconduct behind Pat's death hit the press, it would only draw attention to the war's problems. Whereas if he'd died in the pursuit of a noble goal—saving his fellow servicemen, as his friend Steve White had been told and had repeated to the thousands watching Pat's memorial—well, it would serve the public relations arm of the war effort very nicely. It made me sick that people had tried to twist Pat's virtue to fit a moral narrative of their choosing. But even as I sent in request after request for information, looking for who those people were, I understood that getting stuck in those thoughts wouldn't help my healing.

Shortly after Pat was killed, while I was still living near Fort Lewis, I decided I needed to meet with Greg Baker, the soldier who had issued the "fire" order that day in the canyon. The press had zoomed in on him from the beginning, and I felt compelled to reach out to him, to see him in person, although why, exactly, I couldn't determine. Maybe it was because his life had changed so much that day, too. I really wasn't sure. "Hi, Greg, it's Marie Tillman," I said when he picked up my call.

"Oh. Hello," he answered, clearly caught off guard.

"I was just wondering if you'd be free for coffee—maybe Saturday at ten? I'd just like to talk to you for a minute."

"Um, sure," he finally said.

I suggested a place, and we hung up.

I had met Greg a couple of times before Pat died, at various barbecues and social functions at Fort Lewis. I remembered him as a normal guy, nice enough, who had wanted a long career in the military. Kevin and Pat had considered him a good person and a smart soldier. But I wasn't sure what to expect now.

The coffee shop was filled with people chatting happily, making the purpose of my presence feel a little surreal. I skipped the drink line, sat down at a table, and waited. When Greg walked in, the first thing that struck me was how young he looked. He looked like any of the other college kids in the coffee shop with their open books, studying for exams. He glanced at me quickly, then looked down, then looked at me again. He sat down at the table I'd selected in the back corner and we talked for several minutes. "How are you doing?" he asked.

"It's hard," I said, "but I'm dealing with it."

"I, uh, I'm really sorry about everything that happened," he said.

"Don't you want to get a coffee?" I asked.

"No, that's okay."

"Okay." We were quiet for a minute, neither of us sure where to go next. Finally I asked him to tell me his version of what had happened the day Pat was killed, and he did. It sounded a bit recited and was the same general story the military had fed us. I moved on.

"So what are you going to do now?" I asked.

He told me that he'd be leaving the military, that he

might go back to school. His life had changed considerably, and I actually felt a little sorry for him. We finished our stilted conversation and walked toward the parking lot. I could tell there was something more he wanted to say.

"Tell Kevin..." He wasn't able to finish his sentence, and started to cry.

I was devastated by the loss of Pat, and here I was, talking to one of the guys partially responsible for his death. I wanted to be angry at him, but as he started to cry, I wasn't angry at all. I saw the pain clearly on his face. I reached over and hugged him.

I wouldn't pass his message to Kevin, though. In fact, I'd planned the meeting while Kevin was out of town, knowing how angry he'd be if he knew I was meeting with Greg. Sometimes I wished I could feel angrier, like Kevin did. Anger can be a useful emotion. It can help you get out of bed in the morning; it can help you seek and achieve justice. But for better or for worse, it wasn't the way I was wired. I had always had a hard time being angry with people, because I was usually able to imagine their state of mind, even if I disagreed with it or if it had hurt me. It might have been different if I'd felt Pat had been killed on purpose. But in Greg's case, I felt more than anything that he'd been a scared kid with a gun, and things had gone horribly wrong. My life had changed irrevocably that day, but so had his.

Regardless of how I felt about Greg, a shameful cover-up had taken place, and Pat had died violently. I kept picturing Greg's "fire" order, the bullets penetrating Pat's skull. I shook my head to dislodge the image. This wasn't what I wanted. I wanted to remember him full of life. I wanted back the picture of the last time I'd seen him. After I'd decided to call in sick that last day, we lounged in bed; then I dropped him and Kevin off at Fort Lewis to catch their flight and drove home with a heavy heart. Almost immediately after I walked in the door, Pat called to say their flight had been delayed by a couple of hours, so I turned around and met him at a Starbucks near Fort Lewis. When I dropped him off the second time, he turned back to give one last little wave good-bye. I couldn't find that picture in my head anymore. Instead, images of his last minutes on earth followed me across the country to New York.

The day of my dinner with Kelly and her friends, a couple of forensic experts contacted Dannie and offered to review Pat's autopsy report. I wanted to advance our search for the truth, but I was also suspicious. Since Pat's death, it seemed like hordes of people had descended to offer their assistance when really they were looking to capitalize in some way on Pat's name or image. Reporters, writers, lawyers, filmmakers—everybody wanted in on the Tillman story. It had made me deeply mistrustful and guarded, and I felt the seriousness of my role as the guardian of Pat's legacy each day. He'd trusted me, and I was extremely protective of him. I was afraid that his autopsy was going to get out somehow, or that photos were going to leak and show up on the Internet. I didn't want that for my sake and Pat's family's sake, but I especially didn't want it for Pat's sake. I was figuring it all out as I went, and after some deliberation, I declined to give the forensic experts authorization unless they agreed to sign a nondisclosure agreement.

Alex was an enormous help during this period, fielding calls for me and generally doing whatever he could to protect me. But still, the stream of attorneys, investigators, and journalists, the long calls with Dannie, and the painful paperwork wore on me, slowing down my express train. I wanted them to all go away. Pat was gone, and I needed to focus on accepting a life without him. I kept Pat's good-bye letter to me in a drawer in my bed stand, and on a nearly nightly basis, I would take it out of its envelope and let him tell me to live. He wouldn't want to see me stuck. He wanted me to have a life.

It would be easier to have a life if I could soak up a little sunshine, I reasoned. February in New York City is cold—much colder than in Washington—so when Maura invited me to go to the Caribbean with her and a group of other women, I accepted. We stayed in a beautiful house overlooking the beach, lounged in the sun all day, then danced all night. One night we met a group of young guys, and we danced with them for hours, saying little more over the pulsing music than "Sure, I'll have another Pacifico." I felt light—lighter than I'd felt in a long, long time.

I returned home to find a uniformed officer at my door who wanted to brief me about the next level of investigations into Pat's death—hearings before Congress. My first thought was *Oh god, I hope none of my neighbors saw him.* I didn't want them to ask questions about why a military officer would be waiting to talk to me. I wanted to be their young blonde neighbor who worked in the media and danced on the beach—not a tragic widow mired in investigations.

———

Pat's entire family flew to DC for the congressional hearing, and I met them there. I didn't welcome the scrutiny the hearing had brought back to my life, the constant calls from reporters. I resented the hearings; I resented that I had to be there and listen to people who didn't know Pat talk about him all day. I resented that I was trying to move on with my life and yet the whole lurid affair kept pulling me back to a dark and foggy place. Then I felt guilty for being resentful, and the horrible cycle continued.

I sat behind Kevin as he made the opening statement. He was trying to move forward with his life, too. I hadn't seen him in months. He was living in Phoenix now, working with a friend and trying to find meaning in the leftover scraps of his life. Since we'd vacated our cottage in University Place, we'd talked on the phone occasionally, but not much. The time difference between New York and Phoenix, my demanding job, and busy schedules could all be blamed, but really I think we just needed some space. Our time together after Pat had died had been intense and sad, and it was hard to look at each other and not be reminded of that difficult period. But though seeing him now was still hard, those feelings were nothing compared to the pride I felt watching him speak. Kevin had as much of an aversion to the spotlight as I did—if not more—so I knew how much it must have taken for him to sit down in front of the microphone and cameras.

"After the truth of Pat's death was partially revealed," he said, "Pat was no longer of use as a sales asset and became strictly the Army's problem. They were now left with the task of briefing our family and answering our questions. With any luck, our family would sink quietly into our grief, and the whole unsavory episode would be swept under the rug. However, they miscalculated our family's reaction."

Kevin went on eloquently, and it pained me when he spoke about Pat. "The fact that the Army," he said, "and what appears to be others, attempted to hijack his virtue and his legacy is simply horrific. The least this country can do for him in return is to uncover who is responsible for his death, who lied and who covered it up, and who instigated those lies and benefited from them. Then ensure that justice is meted out to the culpable."

Congressman Henry Waxman headed the committee sponsoring the hearing, and as the hearing closed, he said, "What we have is a very clear, deliberate abuse intentionally done. Why is it so hard to find out who did it?" My sentiments exactly.

When I got back to New York, I called my sister, Christine—who had been watching on C-SPAN at home—to debrief the whole experience. "I can't believe this is my life," I told her, repeating what had become my mantra lately. When all this crap was over, I'd be able to rebuild my life. But was it ever going to be over? We'd learned there was going to be another hearing several months later. I'd have to sit in the hearing room again. I'd have to listen again to details from Pat's autopsy report, to accounts of the days following his death. There was nothing that I wanted less. I could always count on Christine to echo my feelings, usually saying, "I can't believe it's your life, either. This is crazy, it's like you live in a movie." This time, though, she didn't keep to the script. She was quiet a moment.

"But, Marie, it *is* your life," she finally said. "So what are you going to do?"

I didn't say anything. I think I'd been waiting for her

to ask me that simple question, but I didn't know how to answer right then.

———

I'd grown to dread looking in the mirror. I don't consider myself a particularly vain person, but was annoyed that my skin was in a constant angry state of pimpled imperfection, and my hair was falling out in clumps. I had circles under my eyes, because I often spent nights trying to prop myself up to reduce the acid reflux that jarred me awake. *Less coffee*, I vowed. More disturbing to me was that I had no energy. I was completely zapped by the end of the day and often crawled into bed before nine p.m. *More exercise*, I promised. I always felt better when I exercised. I didn't think I had a major disease or anything, but couldn't figure out what the problem was. Here I had a new life, an active life, and I was generally taking care of myself. I couldn't understand why I looked and felt like such crap.

One morning I was flipping through a magazine and ran across an article about a yoga studio and wellness spa not too far from my apartment. I went online to do a little more research and was quickly impressed by their philosophy of wholeness and integration. They touted a multidiscipline approach to whole health as the "key to achieving sustainable transformation." The site promised "a total overhaul." A mind, body, spirit transformation. I pulled on some sweats, threw my hair into a ponytail, and walked the eight blocks to check it out. I pushed open the doors and aromatherapy and soft music swept me up. I immediately felt better. I looked at the menu of programs they provided, and stopped at 6-WEEK TOTAL BODY TRANSFORMATION. I didn't think six weeks was enough, but it was a start and I was desperate. I plunked down the two thousand dollars for the total body transformation, rationalizing that a month's rent was a reasonable price for the promise of serenity. I scheduled appointments with a nutritionist, an acupuncturist, and a masseuse and signed up for a yoga class. I left feeling more hopeful than I had in a while.

Two days later, I returned for my first acupuncture appointment. I was a little squeamish about someone poking me with needles, but willing to give it a try. Lucy, petite with long dark hair and delicate hands, was just what I needed. In our first meeting, she asked me all kinds of questions about my diet, exercise, energy levels, stress. I told her about my skin, fatigue, and hair loss, but I didn't say a word about the real loss I had suffered. That didn't have anything to do with this, I thought. Right after Pat died, I wondered if people could tell just by looking at me that I felt completely altered. I'd thought it must be visible to everyone I came in contact with. Now was different, though. I was out and about in the world. I was working hard, making friends, exercising. Something was wrong, I was sure, but it wasn't grief that was causing my health problems.

"City life can be hectic," Lucy said, "and it sounds like

you're pretty busy traveling with your job. Do you have a lot of stress in your life?"

"Just your basic work-related stuff," I said.

Lucy looked at my tongue.

"Your liver is sluggish," she said. She squinted at my skin. "You should avoid dairy to clear that up."

She asked me to lie down on the table, then put tiny needles into my feet, hands, belly, and forehead, explaining as she went what each was supposed to do. Her soft voice soothed my nerves as she talked about what it was like growing up as a Chinese American, and how she got into acupuncture. I relaxed into her gentle care. Before I left, she placed small silver balls at pressure points on my ears and told me to press gently down on them throughout the week. I didn't notice an immediate change but felt just a bit better as I walked home.

I spent the next six weeks immersed in taking care of myself. I read everything I could about alternative healing and Eastern medicine and quickly became a convert. An on-again, off-again vegetarian since the age of twelve, I cut meat out of my diet, stocking my refrigerator with veggies and fruit. And I looked forward to my time with Lucy every week.

"How was your week?" she asked at our second appointment, as she would at all the appointments that followed. "Was it a good week, or a stressful week?"

"Nothing unusual," I answered, but then I remembered a tense conversation I'd had earlier that day about the investigations. As Lucy gently poked my arms and legs, as we talked about restaurants and movies, I found myself thinking about the hearing. I'd lived in a state of chaos for two years, I realized, so long that it had become my normal, but there was nothing normal about it. Though what was going on would have been obvious to anyone who knew my story, that was the first moment that I connected the physical maladies I'd been experiencing to the stress of the past two years.

When I saw Lucy the next week, I let it drop that I'd been married.

"My husband was killed in Afghanistan," I said.

"Mmmm," Lucy said, and continued gently about her work before saying softly, "I'm sorry to hear that." She left for a moment to dim the lights further, then said, "How long ago?"

"About two years," I said.

Lucy prodded the conversation as gently as she prodded my body, not asking for more than I wanted to say. But I explained everything to her anyway. I told her about the never-ending investigations and hearings that had worn my fragile state of mind completely thin. I told her about how deeply I felt the responsibility of making the right decisions for Pat's legacy. I told her how I dreamed about him often, and how in my dreams, he was usually mad at me—either for not living, or for having fun to the extent that I forgot about him. That day and in the weeks after, when I'd lay on the table, tears would roll down my face as she gently poked me with needles and rubbed my temples.

Touch, I realized through my sessions with Lucy, had been a huge void in my life. I'd heard of the practice of massaging preemie babies because of how crucial human touch is to development, but I'd never thought to apply it to myself. With Pat, I'd taken for granted that I would get cuddled, my hair would be mussed, and I'd receive count-less subtle hugs and squeezes. Now it wasn't like I was going to go around hugging my girlfriends all the time, and I didn't even have that many in New York. With Lucy, and with the spa's masseuse, I was paying for the privilege of being touched and cared for. It didn't feel sad or pathetic, though. It felt empowering. I was learning to take care of myself.

Sunday is my favorite day. Every Sunday in New York, I would brew a big pot of strong coffee, make scrambled eggs, and read through the entire newspaper. It would sometimes be hours before I got out of my pajamas or ran a brush through my hair, and I loved it. One Sunday, I was sitting at my breakfast nook with my favorite mug and the *New York Times* when the phone rang. I saw from the caller ID that it was Dannie. I was about to hit the talk button, then hesitated. I knew how the conversa-tion would go. We'd go over new details she'd discovered in the mounds of testimony and volumes of documents that might help provide a clue to who should be held responsible for the cover-up. I'd hang up the phone and notice new knots in my neck and shoulders, and I'd work on loosening my tightened jaw. Then I'd spend the rest of the day in a funk, too restless to be in my apartment but too sad to leave it.

I didn't want that today—at least, not yet. I needed more time. I needed to take some modicum of control over a completely insane situation.

I wouldn't run from what Dannie wanted to talk about. I'd call her back. But there was no reason I couldn't call her a little later. I let the call go through to voice mail and went back to reading the paper.

CHAPTER SEVEN

I entered a restaurant near Madison Square Garden and found my friend Carolyn at the bar. She was like a cool younger aunt, whisking into town from Phoenix with concert tickets at just the right time. She was always so put together, and fit right in with the upscale after-work crowd. Her shoulder-length dark hair was neatly in place, her shirt crisply professional. She has light blue eyes and, despite the Arizona sun, porcelain skin. I, on the other hand, was a bit disheveled. A steady rain had fallen most of the day and had revealed the natural curl of my blown-straight hair. I felt dingy and out of place.

She smiled and waved to me. She had coaxed me into coming out. She'd said she had an extra ticket to a show, but it was extra because she'd bought it for me.

It was a U2 concert, part of their Vertigo tour. I wasn't really expecting much. I liked their music but had never seen them in concert. Carolyn was a huge U2 fan. She worked in marketing for a major resort in Phoenix, and she helped with the Pat Tillman Foundation. She was currently taking time off from everything and contemplating a job change. She joked about turning into a groupie and following U2 around the East Coast.

We made our way from the restaurant through the crowds of people and dutifully waited in the long security line to get into the Garden. By the time we got to our seats, it was already a few minutes past the scheduled showtime. When the lights went down, and that U2 concert started up—loud, beautiful, with millions of lights, like the Manhattan skyline—it was like the first time I had heard music at all.

I stood up to take it all in; the crowd screamed as Bono began. The force of the music and the crowd was overwhelming. I remember the crowd even more than the music. Thousands of people—all survivors of one kind or another—swayed and sang together under the colored lights. The concert started on a powerful note and kept raising the ante, sending us all higher. At one point, the house lights came up and illuminated the faces in the crowd. At that moment, I was hit with the realization of Bono's power. Everybody wanted to touch the live wire. The power the singer held over the people packed into the stadium was like nothing I had ever seen. He was fully engaged in life and he was in the moment, and people connected with that. I thought about how intoxicating that must be, and what a responsibility it was to command that kind of respect and control.

Leaving the show, Carolyn and I stepped out into the still-rainy night. It was coming down hard. We walked in a trance for a few blocks and then took our separate cabs home. You think life is over, and then something shakes you like that. I was shaken to see that energy again. Energy is what I had lived so long beside. Energy is who I had married—the energy that permeates life, that comes out of every pore and explodes into the world. It was comforting and entirely surprising to see it was still there. And just like that, music—which I had muted for so long in favor of silent contemplation—came back into my life.

———

Several weeks later, all thoughts of music were behind me as I jetted around the country. It seemed I never stayed put in New York for long, and my travel schedule that spring was particularly grueling. I stepped into an airport in the dry heat of Phoenix and stepped out in the dense, humid air of a Miami spring. The Pat Tillman Foundation, which Christine's husband, Alex, was leading, had just put on Pat's Run in Tempe. The run was a major fund-raiser for the foundation and involved around thirty thousand people running 4.2 miles (in honor of Pat's football number, 42). Both my and Pat's families turned out among the runners, as did a slew of old friends, coaches, and teammates. The event was successful, but the weekend left me feeling drained. While I loved being around people who loved Pat so much, I also felt sad. I wanted him to be there, hanging out and running with us. The event also cast me into a very public role once more, and I craved hiding out in the anonymity of my apartment in Manhattan for a little while. A retreat home wasn't in the cards, however, as I was needed in Miami for a work project.

I waited in line for a taxi, then asked to go to the fancy downtown hotel where my colleagues were already working. They had set up camp in the suite of a television producer named J.P., whom I had never met, but who would be working with us on an ESPN prime-time special for the next several months. A lot of hype preceded this meeting, as J.P. was reportedly a pretty powerful, wealthy guy. Rumors painted him as a charmer and a lothario, as a huge presence in every room he entered. He was also an incredibly gifted businessman. We were certain to learn a lot from him, people said, and we started to feel a bit privileged to be given the opportunity.

Under normal circumstances, the hype might have made me nervous. But with Pat's Run so close to my consciousness, I didn't really have enough energy for the emotion. When I walked into the hotel suite, the first thing that struck me was what a respite the cool, conditioned air was from the oppressive heat outside. I was also floored by the suite's enormity. With keyboards clacking and printers humming all around, it felt like an upscale office. Only the open bedroom door revealing the elegant king-sized bed indicated that this wasn't exclusively a workplace. J.P. hadn't arrived yet, so after chatting with colleagues for a minute or two, I found a comfortable corner of the floor, pulled out my laptop, and started to catch up on email, willing myself back into work mode.

I looked up when I heard a flurry of activity, guessing, correctly, that J.P. had arrived. At first glance, he didn't seem that intimidating. He looked to be somewhere in his thirties, had cropped blond hair and blue eyes, and was wearing jeans and a fitted cotton T-shirt. Then I caught sight of the entourage that followed him in— easily five or six people, who were clearly attentive to his every movement and mood. *Is this how power is built?* I wondered. *Get a few people to fawn and then everyone thinks they're supposed to?* I waved hello when I heard someone pointing me out to him, then turned my attention back to my email.

After a few minutes, J.P. came over and stood directly in front of where I was sitting on the floor. He knelt down and extended his hand. "Hi," he said, smiling. "We didn't really have a proper introduction. I'm J.P." His eyes were bluer than they'd looked from a distance, and he had a boyish way about him. There was something magnetic in his presence, and suddenly my stomach flipped.

"I thought we'd have the formal part of the meeting in the conference room downstairs," he said. "Are you ready? We can walk down together."

"Sure, yes," I said. I stood up and awkwardly collected my things while he waited. We chatted easily as we walked to the elevator bank, and I was struck by how unassuming he was, with his thick southern accent and relaxed demeanor. He didn't seem like a bigwig producer; he definitely had an aura, but he also seemed like a cool, nice guy.

"A bunch of us are going to go for dinner later," I said, making small talk. "Any recommendations?"

"What kind of food do you guys want?"

"We're not picky. What are some unique Miami places?"

He listed a few places to eat, but I was so distracted by his presence they barely registered. *I'm just being polite,* I thought. *I'm not nervous; I'm just making conversation because that's what people do when they're in an elevator together.* But there was something more going on. I just wasn't sure what. I did know that I felt like a schoolgirl.

I didn't want to be attracted to this man. It wasn't the right time, I wasn't in the right place, and of all people to feel attracted to, he certainly shouldn't be the one—a playboy with a known predilection for blondes. I didn't want this. I sat through the business meeting, trying to avoid looking at him, trying not to notice him looking at me, trying to ignore that everyone was vying for his attention. Still, by the time we said good-bye that first day, I was pretty sure that whatever I felt was out of my control.

———

Pat had been gone over two years, and by then people were encouraging me to date. My mom's friends were always telling me how they hated seeing a young girl alone so much. I imagined that I could date then if I wanted to; it might be healthy. But I hadn't dated since I was fifteen, and outside of fielding the constant encouragement to get back out there, I didn't think about it much. I worried that as the widow, I was going to be something of a broken girl in the social scene.

The more I talked with my single girlfriends at the office and in my building, the more I came to realize that nearly everyone was a little damaged, one way or another. And that I had once had a great love, and knew what that felt like, was maybe less damaging than having suffered a long string of less meaningful relationships. I was not down on men or love. The city had not pounded cynicism into my heart. I knew how to give love and receive it. I kept that affirmation going in my mind. I was not broken. I would not think of myself in that way. I would not allow myself to be buried with my husband, as some ancients were; I would overcome the mental equivalent of the funeral pyre. I would unfold Pat's letter and let him tell me again to please have a life.

A couple of times I'd sensed interest from men. Usually I was the last one to notice it, and the first one to panic. Once a friend of a friend came to town and the three of us hung out. We chatted easily all night, and when he emailed me the next week from his home in Chicago, I didn't think much about it. I emailed him back, and we started a friendly email banter. Then one day he wrote that he was considering coming out to New York for another visit, even though our mutual friend wouldn't be there. Would I be available for dinner? I was caught totally off guard, and deleted the email without responding. The poor guy got the point and backed off.

It probably didn't help my romantic life any that I was still wearing my wedding ring. I just didn't feel ready to take it off. It also felt like an act of defiance; my mom's friends and the rest of the world thought if I had fun and had a boyfriend, that would mean I'd moved on. My ring was a reminder that I was not over it, and it wasn't fair to ask me to be. With my ring firmly in place, no one could question my continued commitment to Pat. This little band placed on the third finger of the left hand held great meaning. Wedding rings have been exchanged for centuries, the circle symbolizing eternity—no beginning, no end.

It also happened to be beautiful. Sometime after Pat

gave it to me, I was admiring it aloud to him. "Don't get used to it," he'd teased. "That's the last piece of nice jewelry you're ever getting."

My grandma had her own solution to the ring problem. She had moved her wedding ring from her left to her right hand after my grandpa died, and twenty-five years later, it still remained there. One day when I was living in Washington, I'd tried out this approach, placing my engagement ring and wedding band on my right hand. While they easily slid over my left knuckle, I had to wiggle them onto my right finger. The weight felt strange on this hand, but I tried to get used to it. I went about my day, not thinking much about it until I was checking out at the grocery store. The young clerk ringing up my groceries said, "Isn't your wedding ring on the wrong hand?"

I fumbled over myself. "Uh, oh yeah. I guess it is." I was embarrassed and a little angry. But it was a fair question. People wouldn't automatically assume that I, at twenty-seven, was widowed because my wedding ring was on my right hand. Once I'd moved my groceries into the back of the car, I replaced my rings on my left hand. There was no easy transition, literally or physically. The ring was either on or off, and I wasn't ready to take it off.

———

It was several weeks before I saw J.P. again, and I talked myself into believing the initial flirtation had existed only in my imagination. He hadn't paid me any special attention that day, I thought. I had only imagined he had smiled just a bit more at me, or met my eye across the conference table more than he'd met anyone else's.

At our next meeting, and the several that followed immediately, his attention grew harder to cast aside, even for someone as clueless as I often was. He seemed to make a point of seeking me out and asking me how I was doing. I didn't notice him doing that with anyone else. My colleagues were starting to grin knowingly at me when J.P.'s back was turned. Many times when he came over to me to chat, it began with a business question but then turned into a long conversation about running, or travel, or our favorite places to eat in New York City. Then one day I was waiting in line for coffee when I got a text from him. I hadn't given him my number, I thought, and realized he must have sought it out.

In NYC this weekend, he wrote. *Meet us for sushi?*

Meet *us.* Of course there was an *us,* as J.P. never went far without his entourage. The group took the pressure off, though. I didn't have to read his message as a request for a formal date. He was just going to be in town, hanging out with a group of people, and since we were now friends, I guessed, of course it made sense that he would ask me along. And there was no reason I shouldn't go, I thought. He was a nice guy, and it wasn't like we would be alone. *Sure,* I texted back.

I felt funny about the possibility of anything happening or anyone else at work knowing about our flirtation. We worked together. He was powerful in the entertainment industry. He'd just been through a breakup, and he had a couple of kids. How could it be even remotely professional for us to get too friendly? I might find him attractive, but I wasn't ready for something like this. All these schoolgirl emotions had caught me completely off guard in the first place. But it was a nice distraction. Most of the time I felt stressed or sad, so it felt good to have a few butterflies to add to the mix. Was that really so bad?

The night we met up for sushi was fun and casual, and it was nice to hang out in a nonprofessional capacity, although our work relationship was never far from my mind. We saw each other even more frequently as the project we were working on heated up. Always it was the same: "Hey, Marie, how's it going?" he'd say, then find something small to tease me about—that he could surely kick my butt in a game of Ping-Pong, or that I was all work and no play. He never asked about my past, or asked too deeply about my life, but I knew he knew about Pat. The fratricide news was still all over the papers, and my boss eventually confessed that she had told him my story when he'd inquired after our first meeting in Miami.

When the project was over, I felt a huge letdown. Surely I wouldn't cross paths with J.P. anymore. In some ways it was good that I wouldn't spend any more mental energy thinking about him, but in other ways, I would miss it.

We texted casually over the next few weeks, but less frequently. In one exchange I wrote that I was headed to L.A. for work, and he wrote right back, *Me too. Meet up with us?*

Okay, I thought. *There's no professional reason to meet up or continue an in-person relationship. I know it and he knows it. But why not? It'll be a big group of people; we'll hang out and have fun.* Maybe something would happen, maybe not. I was going to play it cool. I wasn't going to do what I saw many of my girlfriends do in situations like these: I wasn't going to overthink it.

Almost immediately after I showed up at the club, Hyde, my interaction with J.P. felt different. Without the work project between us, it felt like a more serious flirtation. He was sharing his table with a group of seven or so friends that night, and we drank and danced until the early hours of the morning. When J.P. suggested we go back to one of his friends' houses in the Hollywood Hills for more drinks, even with my light buzz, I knew something would probably happen.

When we kissed that night, all I could think about was how unfamiliar this man was. That didn't mean I wasn't excited, but I couldn't help comparing him to Pat. Even though it was different, I found myself leaning into the comfort of his body. I realized how much I had missed this closeness, and even with this relative stranger, my body reacted.

We'd been playing a game, and we both knew it. What's

more, we somehow both knew the rules. This would be casual; this would be fun. We had a mutual attraction, but we lived in different cities. We also both had a lot of other stuff going on, and a serious relationship wouldn't make sense. I knew any sort of involvement would be casual, and I wanted it anyway.

Just the same, the excitement of the encounter left me in a giddy daze. When I got back to New York, I had to tell someone. I called Christine.

"Hey, it's me," I said. "What's up?"

"Today was such a nightmare," she said, spilling over. "I'm exhausted. Scott's been sick and was up all night." She launched into a story about the chaos of her life at home with three young kids. While usually I listened actively and empathized, that day I couldn't contain myself. I cut her off mid-sentence.

"I met someone," I blurted out.

"What? What do you mean you met someone?"

I explained it all, how we had met in Miami and how I had been instantly drawn to him but thought I must be mistaken about his interest. I rambled on for several minutes about the texts, about Hyde, about going to his friend's house afterward. When I was done, there was silence on the other end.

"Hello? Christine? Are you still there?"

"Wait a second," she said. There was a long pause before she spoke again. "I don't know if I'm ready for this."

"I know!" I practically shrieked. "If you're not ready for this, how do you think *I* feel?"

I instantly understood what Christine meant. Pat had been not only in my life, but also in hers. For eleven years he'd been a big part of our family. Since he had died, she'd mostly focused on me, but I knew she was also dealing with her own devastation and grief.

"It's just strange for me to think of you with someone else," she said.

"I can't imagine myself with anyone else, either," I said, "but I'm just attracted to this guy. I can't really explain it." I swore her to secrecy. I didn't want anyone else to know. It was too soon. Even I didn't understand why I was feeling this way. How could anyone else?

———

This affair was ideal, I thought. It was the perfect way to ease myself back into dating. I knew it wouldn't be too serious, so there was no pressure, and that was exactly what I needed to feel comfortable. We flirted unmercifully when we saw each other, and flirted even more over text while we were apart. I felt young and light. Sitting alone at night in my apartment, I'd hear my phone buzz and see it was a text from him. *Thinking of you...* I would be instantly lifted by the excitement of this little note. I felt so beat up that on some level, I had questioned whether anyone would ever find me attractive again. So in the beginning, a simple "thinking of you" message would leave me glowing for days.

J.P. lived on a large estate in Charleston, and after we'd gone out in New York a few more times, he invited me to fly down to spend the weekend with him. I didn't hesitate more than a heartbeat before agreeing. "I'm locked into a business dinner on Friday night," he said, "so I'll be having some people over. But I think you'll have fun—it'll be a good group."

It was fine with me; I was now used to tagging along to whatever event or meeting or dinner he had in New York, so a Charleston event wouldn't feel much different. When we first started seeing each other, I was a little uncomfortable in these situations, wondering if anyone present would know my story or wonder what was going on. But J.P. made everything easier. He had a comfortable way about him, and I noticed that most of the people he surrounded himself with followed his lead. He never introduced me by my full name, and most people assumed I was his latest girlfriend and didn't put much more thought into it. Feeling secure that my true identity was concealed, I became more comfortable chatting with his associates. I was always polite but vague when asked about myself. In fact, I had it down to a science. I could talk about my job and living in New York for hours if someone was particularly inquisitive. I could easily seem like just another young professional and leave out all the complicated past.

I landed in Charleston Friday evening, took a car to his place, and tried to make myself presentable after the flight while he greeted his guests. I came out from the back bedroom and wandered over to the bar to get a drink. Glass of wine in hand, I was checking out the small crowd when a tall, younger guy with a mop of dark hair came over to me.

"Hi, I'm John," he said.

"Hey, nice to meet you. I'm Marie."

"I think we have a friend in common," he said.

My heartbeat sped up. "We do?"

"Yeah, Brian Shaw."

"Oh," I said, trying to sound light and casual. "Sure, I know Brian." Inside, I was terrified. Brian had been one of Pat's trainers in college. How did this guy know who I was? How did he know the connection? I felt totally exposed and suddenly became incredibly self-conscious. Was John going to tell Brian I was seeing J.P.? Did Brian already know? Did other people know? What about Pat's family? What if they found out? I had carefully guarded this relationship so far, telling myself it was not going to go anywhere serious, so why upset everyone?

I wanted to run away from John as fast as possible, but instead I chatted brightly and tried to turn the subject away from our common friend. The rest of the night was miserable. I tried to maintain a calm exterior, but I was frantic inside, realizing the carefully constructed facade that I had created was starting to crumble. After the last guest had left, J.P. sat down on the couch beside me. I was normally chatty and engaging, but that night I couldn't put the energy into starting a conversation.

"You seem quiet tonight. Are you okay?" he asked. It was the perfect opportunity to open up to him, to explain what I was going through.

"Just tired," I said, and asked him how he felt the party had gone. We chatted casually for a while, then went to bed.

I'd been finding it difficult to concentrate on work lately, and things were falling through the cracks. I didn't want to get any further behind, so the afternoon after the party, I sat at J.P.'s kitchen counter with my laptop, trying to catch up. I quickly surveyed my email, responding to the most pressing issues. My phone buzzed and I saw it was Dannie. I stared at it for a moment. Had she heard from Brian? Did she know? I shook off the thought, realizing I was being crazy. J.P. was down the hall in his office, doing some work of his own, but I didn't feel like I could talk to Dannie while he was in earshot. I picked up the phone and opened the back patio door so I could talk freely outside. Beyond the covered patio, past an expanse of perfectly maintained lawn, were a few steps leading to another patio. I walked across the lawn and sat down on the steps.

"Hey there," Dannie said warmly. "How are you? *Where* are you?"

"I'm good," I said. "I'm in Charleston for a few

days." Since starting my job at ESPN, I'd traveled constantly, and my friends and family back home really didn't know what I was up to, and no longer asked. They would probe a little bit about what my life was like, but I'd answer in vague terms, and after several rounds of this, they settled with the fact that I was working a lot and keeping myself busy. So when I told Dannie I was in Charleston, this half-truth didn't solicit any follow-up questions. She assumed it was work-related and went on to explain why she had called.

"I'm working on my book and I wanted to share a section with you," she said. She'd decided to write about her pursuit of justice amid the fratricide cover-up. I thought the book would be a great thing for her, and I could tell she was excited. I wanted to be supportive.

"Great, go ahead," I said.

She started to read, to describe sitting in front of her house, watching the glow from her fire pit and thinking about Pat. She wrote about feeling crippling loss, about feeling exposed. I had spent many nights by that fire pit in front of her house, watching Pat goof around with his brothers, or just talking to him, and we'd even had our rehearsal dinner near that fire pit. It was the place Pat's closest family and friends had congregated right after he'd died. The memories, close to the surface, broke through. Tears welled up in my eyes and silently spilled over and down my cheeks. What she had written was beautiful, her pain of the loss of Pat eloquently voiced, her agony clear. When she finished, I told her how moving I thought it was, and marveled at her ability to express her feelings when I was still struggling with my own. I, too, had started writing after Pat died, in an attempt to free some of the emotion that suffocated me. But unlike Dannie's, my words came out in a jumbled mess, long pages of stream of consciousness that made little sense. We hung up the phone and I sat for a few minutes, looking back at J.P.'s enormous house, conflicted. Dannie was so open, so trusting in her willingness to share her writing. I felt like I was lying to her by not sharing this new part of my life. I wondered if J.P. could see me sitting here in the yard, silently crying.

I couldn't help wondering what would happen if I let J.P. see me, if I exposed this side. From our initial meeting until then, I had kept my life compartmentalized. We never spoke about Pat, or about the fratricide investigations. I never let my two worlds collide. I felt it was not something he wanted to discuss, but neither did I. I wanted things to stay light and fun and at the surface. I wasn't ready to have someone in my life, really in the deep dark recesses of it.

I wiped my eyes and took a few deep breaths. When I walked back into the kitchen, J.P. was poking around in the refrigerator. "Want to go get some lunch?" he asked cheerily.

"Sure!" I beamed back.

———

"What is your problem?" Christine asked me over the phone the next week.

"What are you talking about?" I had just confided in her about running into John at the party in Charleston and fearing that word had gotten out.

"Do you really think Pat's family would be upset? You know they want you to be happy."

"I know," I said, and I did. "I don't know, I guess I just feel guilty. Like I shouldn't be with someone else. You know? It's like I have this voice inside my head telling me it's too soon."

"Marie," Christine said, gentler now. "You're being way too hard on yourself. What advice would you give a friend going through this? Would you tell her she should wait ten years?"

"No, of course not," I said. "But I don't know what the appropriate time is—it's not like there's a rule manual for this stuff."

"Fair enough," Christine said, "but what would you tell her?"

"To go easy on herself," I said.

"Well?"

164

My sister was right, and it meant more coming from her than from almost anyone, since I knew what Pat had meant to her. But words alone couldn't change things. I didn't think I could all of a sudden start being gentle with myself. I was stuck in a middle place between the past and a future I couldn't quite make out.

———

J.P. was telling me something over the music, but I couldn't hear him.

"What?" I asked.

"Do you want another drink?" he asked again, louder.

"Oh! Sure!" I said. J.P. and I were with seven other people, sharing a booth at one of the New York clubs whose long lines I used to pass on my way home from working late.

He held up a hand, and it seemed like magically our server appeared out of thin air. Had she been watching our table all along from behind a hidden wall or something, waiting for J.P. to raise an arm? It was weird, but then again, there were a lot of new things I'd discovered since I'd started hanging out with J.P. Like how freeing it was to let loose and dance on a table with friends I'd just met. Like how easy it was to be absorbed into someone else's circle, and to have him take care of everything. Like how far away the crap of my life felt when I was hanging out until two and three a.m. J.P.'s life was big—enormous, really—and in some ways I wanted to be swallowed up into that. I was tired of trying to find my way, tired of everything being so difficult, and in J.P. I saw a way out.

It was after three a.m. when J.P. and I left the club and climbed into the black SUV that was waiting for us outside.

"Since my hotel's across town, should we just go to your apartment tonight?" J.P. suggested. "It's just a few blocks away, right?"

"Oh," I said, and willed myself to sound calm. "Nah, it's really small, and it's a complete mess, since I've been traveling so much." I was panicked at the thought of him in my space. My apartment was my sacred sanctuary. The sight of it would reveal way more of my internal workings than I was willing to share. I couldn't imagine what he would think about the dozens of photos of Pat lining my walls, or the stacks of books I pored over in my darkest times, looking for a hint of inspiration and guidance. A person's space reveals a great deal about him or her, and mine was a treasure map through my troubled psyche. In my cramped one-bedroom apartment, there would be no place to hide the darker parts from a casual visitor.

"Okay, then," J.P. said, and gave the driver the name of his hotel.

I woke up early the next morning, quietly snuck out, and took a cab back to my place, still wearing my dress from the night before, hoping I wouldn't run into anyone I knew. As soon as I got home, I stepped out of my clothes and into the shower. I felt awful. Partying late into the night, talking to people I didn't really know about nothing in particular, felt wrong. It was supposed to be fun but it wasn't me. Having a casual relationship with someone like J.P. wasn't me. I needed to feel a more meaningful connection that just wasn't there, but I didn't want to stop seeing him, so I convinced myself that the distraction was good. Though I was committed to playing it cool, deep down I knew I needed more.

———

"Please, have a seat in the conference room to your left," a congressional aide said, and motioned Pat's family and me through a doorway. "We'll call you to come in shortly." We were in Washington, DC, for the second congressional hearing about the fratricide cover-up. *It ends here*, I thought. *Somehow or other.* I didn't know that we'd feel satisfied with the result, but this was the last stop. There was no higher court or place to go.

Donald Rumsfeld appeared in order to testify, and there had been quite a bit of media leading up to this hearing. I felt the cameras on us immediately after we were called to take our seats in the hearing room.

The final hearing was an outrage. When Rumsfeld testified, he said he couldn't remember when he was first notified about the fratricide. How could that be? He had written Pat a personal letter once he'd enlisted, commending his decision. Rumsfeld had also sent a colleague a memo about how Pat was someone to watch, how he was special. Pat had wanted to be treated like any other serviceman, but he never had been, and there was no way that the implications of the fratricide would have been lost on Rumsfeld. All he said was "I know I would not be involved in a cover-up...I know the gentlemen sitting next to me are men of enormous integrity and would not participate in something like that."

Every fiber of my being was crying *Bullshit!* but I kept a stone face while remaining rigid and unmoving in my seat. One after another, the generals testified that they didn't remember anything. And worse, the congressmen and congresswomen who questioned them seemed ready to let them off the hook, praising them for their service and making the whole affair an opportunity to show how patriotic they were, how appreciative they were of our military leaders. So it's patriotic to lie to the public about how a soldier was killed? Though I had tried to come prepared for anything, I couldn't believe this was where all Dannie's hard work, all the phone calls and Freedom of Information Act requests and investigators and energy, had led us. It was a mockery, and I was furious.

And the next day I'd be back in New York, living my new life and waiting to hear from J.P.

———

I traveled south again the following weekend, this time passing DC in the air en route to Charleston. J.P. had his kids with him for the weekend, and it had tripped me up a little when he'd told me.

"Are you sure about this?" I'd asked on the phone one night, when we were setting it up.

"Yeah, it'll be great," he said. "We can go to the beach house for part of it. It'll be a great time."

"Okay, if you're sure," I said, and booked my ticket.

The weekend was wonderful. The first afternoon, we headed to the beach house and went ATV-ing with his kids—a little boy and girl, both under the age of eight. They were warm and friendly toward me and didn't seem to think too much about why I was there. After the ATV ride, we decided to hike on the beach for a bit. J.P.'s daughter got tired and asked me if I'd give her a piggyback ride, which I happily did. As we bounced along, she chatted comfortably with me, pointing out things she saw along our way.

"So are you spending the night?" she asked after a while, when we'd run out of birds to identify and crab shells to spot.

"Um, yeah, I am."

"Cool," she said. "Where are you gonna sleep?"

I glanced at J.P., who was running a bit ahead of us with his son. He hadn't heard. This was definitely one for him to field, not me.

"Oh," I said, "I'm not really sure. Hey, want to collect some seashells?"

"Sure!" she said brightly, and I set her down. We both searched the sand for shells, the question forgotten.

That night, we ate dinner on the patio outside J.P.'s house, the ocean breeze a welcome respite from the heat, the lapping waves still in view. J.P. and I drank margaritas and ate barbecued chicken while the kids ran around on the surrounding lawn. They'd stop their play every so often to come over and climb on J.P. for a bit. It was clear that he was a great dad, and that his kids adored him. I leaned back in my chair and soaked happily in the domestic scene around me. This was not my home, these were not my kids, and J.P. and I weren't even close to being serious about each other. But I couldn't help thinking how nice, how comfortable it all was. How close it was to the future Pat and I had imagined. My last morning at the beach with J.P., we stayed in bed as long as possible. I snuggled under his arm and put my head on his chest. I liked the feeling of being close to someone again, lingering in bed. He took my hand and laced his fingers through mine.

"You're not wearing your wedding ring," he said. "How come?"

"I guess I don't feel married anymore," I said.

My wedding ring had come off in stages. I'd taken my engagement ring off six months prior but hadn't felt ready to let go of the thin wedding band, the last physical symbol of our marriage. I had been sneaking around with J.P. for months, and it was true that I no longer felt married. But psychologically, there was still so much tied up in this small piece of jewelry. I didn't want to take it off, but for some reason, the week before the beach trip, I felt like it was time. I was in New York, my normal routine in motion. I woke up, went to the gym, showered, and got dressed for work. But that morning when I picked up my ring to put it on before leaving the house, something made me stop. I held it up, feeling the small diamonds between my fingers.

Standing in my bedroom, looking at this beautiful ring that I loved, I knew there was no right answer. I could wear it forever, or take it off. Neither would bring Pat back or prove my love for him. As with many small and large things I had been forced to face since Pat's death, it was up to me to decide the meaning. I pulled a small blue pouch from my jewelry box and took out my engagement ring. I slipped both rings over my left finger. As I held up my hand, the solitaire diamond of my engagement ring caught the morning light coming through the bedroom window, and I wiggled my hand a bit, making it dance. After a few seconds, I slipped both rings off, placed them gingerly in the blue velvet pouch, and tucked it into the back of my drawer. I headed out the door, feeling a strange mix of sadness and resolve.

———

The week after the Charleston trip, I didn't hear much from J.P. A spotty text message or two, and I started agonizing over what they meant. I felt sure the whole thing was falling apart, and I became crazed.

Late at night I would call my sister for advice.

"I haven't heard from him in a couple days. What do you think I should do? Should I call?"

I couldn't believe what I was saying. How had I gotten to this place?

To the outside world, I seemed normal. But in my head I was going crazy, thinking about J.P. all the time. Christine was the only person who knew my real mental state, and she was equally unprepared for handling the situation. Both of us had married our high school boyfriends. We had no experience dating as adults. I felt completely confused and out of sorts. Mostly, I was mad at myself for getting so anxious over this man when so much had happened in my life that was much more real.

We hadn't made a plan for when we would see each other again, and I felt like he had all the power in the situation. I wanted to play it cool, but was it fair for me to have to sit around and wait for him to text me? I didn't want to juggle everything just because he waited too long to tell me he was going to be in town. When J.P. did come to New York again, I asked him straight out, after dinner one night, where he thought this was going.

"What are you talking about?" he said lightly. "I'll give you a call next week. Maybe we can meet up when you're in California for work at the end of the month. Have you ever been to Gjelina in Venice?"

I should have known right then, but for some reason, I convinced myself that I didn't need anything from him. I could go back to being content with just a fun weekend here and there.

"I'm just not sure about this guy," Christine finally said after listening to me relay our flow of communication over the past several days. In our last couple of conversations, I had started to get the feeling that she was suspicious of J.P.'s intentions. She didn't care who he was; she didn't like how he was treating me or the way it was affecting me.

"But it's casual, he doesn't owe me anything, he hasn't done anything wrong, really," I said, feeling a little defensive.

"That doesn't matter," Christine said. "All that matters is whether or not this is good for you. Is it?"

There was no denying that it wasn't good for me, but I wasn't ready to let it go. As my work trip to California neared, I still hadn't heard from J.P. about a definitive plan for meeting up. I felt crazy trying to figure out the point in the relationship when he started pulling away. I kept replaying our last weekend in New York, wondering where it had gone wrong or what I had said that had started to make him distant. I had been moody and a little quiet, tired of spending time with him and then feeling confused when I barely heard from him between visits. I thought that introducing me to his kids and letting me into his life meant that he was interested in more than just casual dating.

The night before I left for California, I called him. To my surprise, he picked up right away.

"So what's up?" I asked, and both he and I knew what I meant.

"Oh, you know," he said. "Marie, you know my track record—I'm just not sure I'm capable of a relationship."

"Right," I said. *It's not you; it's me. Message received.* "Okay, have a good time in California. I'll see you around."

And that was it. A minute-long conversation, and it was done. Then again, maybe that was appropriate for the end of a casual relationship—I wouldn't know. The next couple of weeks I was devastated, but too embarrassed to talk to my sister or any of the few friends who knew we were dating. I had maintained a cool front with all of them except Christine, saying J.P. and I were just hanging out—no big deal, and certainly nothing serious. They assumed I was just having fun, and I didn't think they would understand my devastation. I admonished myself for mourning the loss of this man I barely knew, but soon realized I was mourning something more important than the unraveling of this short-lived relationship.

I had gotten lost in the notion of what J.P. represented, lost in the realization that all these feelings I thought were dead inside me were very much alive. I still wanted to share my life with someone. I wanted the kids running around on the lawn; I wanted the future that Pat and I had talked about, and that I'd glimpsed again that weekend on the beach with J.P. I wanted to journey through life as part of a pair and create a world around us that was deep and meaningful.

Pat's unwavering presence in my life for eleven years had grounded me through all life's ups and downs. Since he'd been killed, I had become caught up in the waves of life and been tossed and turned with nothing to tie me down. I realized that I wanted a connection to another person to anchor my existence, and the realization of this, more than the loss of J.P., caused me to mourn all over again. This notion scared me, because I felt that I had no control. I might meet someone; I might not. All I could do was open the door. As painful as it was to feel so exposed, I promised myself I would keep my heart open to the possibility of love.

In the end, I understood that of course my brief encounter with J.P. had meant more to me than it had to him. There were things he could have handled better. But

I felt grateful for him, because he allowed me to see how much I still valued love.

———

One fall evening not long after J.P. had left my life, I was working late, waiting to meet a colleague in the lobby of the Hudson Hotel in Midtown. The lobby was overgrown, roofed with vine-covered glass, and walking in felt a bit like walking into your entangled, erotic subconscious. In the rosy-paneled library bar by the elevators, a young, dark-haired man sat reading in a large chair below the two stories of bookshelves. Something about him caught my eye: the shaved head, the way he held himself. I had come to recognize the look of a soldier. My suspicions were confirmed when I saw the memorial bracelet around his wrist. I looked down, seeing the gleam of silver around my own wrist. I had been given this bracelet, inscribed with Pat's name, his unit, and the date he'd been killed, after he'd died. It was a constant reminder that I never took off.

As I leaned against the wall, waiting to meet my coworker, I watched the man read for a minute. I was strangely drawn to him. For some reason, surrounded by the fantasy world of the Hudson, I wanted him to know that I was not blind to the realities of the world beyond these wood-paneled walls. I could relate just a little to what he had been through. All that I had been trying to escape by moving to New York was sitting right in front of me, and I wanted to connect, if only for an instant, to the past.

I walked over and the man looked up. I smiled and asked him if he had lost someone in Iraq or Afghanistan. It may seem like an odd way to start a conversation, but when you have been through extreme circumstances, which I assumed he had, niceties like small talk lose their place.

"Yes. A few," he replied. His eyes were intense. He had served in Iraq as a member of the Florida Guard, he said.

He looked at me for a moment.

"And you?" he asked.

"My husband."

There wasn't the look of pity or horror this statement typically provoked. Just two people understanding the reality of each other.

"Wait here," he said. He bolted up and disappeared into an elevator. He returned with a book.

"I wrote this. I want you to have it, in case it might do you any good somehow."

The book was *The Last True Story I'll Ever Tell*, and the young author was John Crawford. I thanked him, tucked the book into my purse, and turned around to find my coworker. Later I read the book, which was an excellent, honest portrayal of life in a war zone. But that wasn't the most significant piece of the encounter. Rather, I saw that the barrier had fallen down. As I'd stood in the Hudson, in my new city, waiting to meet my colleague, who knew nothing of my former life, it had felt oddly comfortable to let my old story wash over me. It was a part of me. Too many times over the past year I had felt like a fraud, shedding my past in search of a future. I couldn't outrun my memories; they weren't going to let me go. I had tucked them away so as not to live in the past, but I now realized I needed to find a way to live comfortably with them in the present.

I'd been lying. Lying to J.P. by pretending I was some carefree fun girl, lying to Pat's family about the light that was starting to shine in my life, and lying to myself, thinking I could keep all these parts of my life separate. The new city, the new job, and even the attempt at dating, all outward signs of progress and forward movement, were a lie. I wanted to take only the good things, the things I thought people could handle, the things I could handle, and carry those into my future, but it doesn't work that way. It wouldn't work that way for me. How could I ever have a relationship or a future without being honest about my past? Before I could be in a relationship, I needed to work through some of the things that I had carefully packed away.

The next morning, I went jogging in Central Park and stopped to look at the autumn leaves swirling around me. This season in New York was over. The city, I felt, had done what I had asked it to do. I was a California girl. My family was there. Pat's foundation was near there. I felt a pull homeward, but in a healthy, new way. Tears filled my eyes as I jogged, because I felt love for this park and this city and what it, and its people, had given me. But it was time to go. When I got home, I called my sister.

"The autumn leaves this morning are unbelievable," I told her.

"What's up?" she yawned. It was too early for her; I had forgotten the time difference again. But she forced herself awake as I talked.

We talked for an hour. She had the best idea: I could move to California without getting caught up in the old shadows, and also be closer to the foundation in Arizona, if I settled in L.A. instead of the Bay Area. It seemed brilliant. I was excited. I am a gypsy and like to move, but this time I was moving not in emotional desperation but in happy anticipation. I didn't know what was out there for me, but I knew what was inside me now, and it was a heart beating toward the future.

One of my favorite underlined passages in Pat's copy of *Self-Reliance* read "Insist on yourself. Never imitate."

Simple, strong, and clear advice. It was time for me to live as Emerson suggested, to be true to who I was. All of me.

PART 3: 2007–2010

Tip the world over on its side and everything loose
will land in Los Angeles.

—Frank Lloyd Wright

CHAPTER EIGHT

My Realtor, Josh, pulled up outside the condo I'd rented in Santa Monica, and I climbed into his black BMW. I'd met Josh through my good friend Matt, and as we chatted in the car, I thought they sort of looked alike, with their short, dark hair and lean, athletic builds. Josh was young and smart, and having spent a number of years in Los Angeles, he had a good grasp of the real estate market and the neighborhoods I would like.

"Ready for round four?" he asked.

"I'm ready," I said, and meant it. I'd really enjoyed the past few weekends of winding around the streets of West Hollywood. At first I had considered staying near the beach, in Venice or Santa Monica. Since I'd returned to California, I'd made a frequent practice of running on the beach, relishing the fact that if I were still in New York, I'd be ducking my chin into my thick wool coat to avoid the harsh, windy winter bite. Romantic beach runs gave way to practicality, however, and I decided to narrow my search to Hollywood so I'd be closer to work and avoid the notorious Los Angeles traffic. After I'd spent many years moving around the country, there was a part of me that wanted to settle in and find a place to call home. So far I'd lived in Los Angeles only three months, and still felt like a visitor instead of a resident. But there was another part of me that felt incredibly anxious at the thought of anything permanent. What if I didn't like it there? What if the arid climate, Santa Ana winds, and absence of seasons made me want to move to another city? I negotiated these conflicting voices and reasoned that, nomadic tendencies aside, a small place that needed some work might be a good investment opportunity. Worst-case scenario, if I decided I wanted to leave Los Angeles, I could always rent the house out once I'd remodeled it. My parents had built a few homes while I was growing up, and I'd been an interested observer when Christine undertook a huge remodel. A little fixer-upper didn't seem that overwhelming, and might tap into some of my creative side, which had lain pretty dormant.

As Josh and I made our way through West Hollywood and up Laurel Canyon, the landscape shifted a bit. There was more space, fewer people. Houses were still clustered

together, but not as packed in as in the flat part of
Hollywood. We drove up to the top of a large hill, wound
around a bit through hairpin turns, and ended up on a
small street with pink bougainvillea dotting nearly every home. We weren't too far away from the city, but
it felt like a world away. It was quiet up here, with an
eclectic mix of houses that seemed as though they'd been
haphazardly thrown up onto the hillside. Many of them
looked like they'd been renovated, but a few were still in
desperate need of a makeover.

The house for sale was situated just off the street and
had an ivy-covered wall and a small gate leading to a
courtyard. The garden was terribly overgrown, with the
ivy strangling everything. We walked in through the
front door to get a look at the interior. A plush rug was
thrown into the entryway, and a simple table with fresh
flowers drew my eye to the far window. The owner had
clearly tried to make the place presentable to get the most
out of potential buyers, but it was still pretty run down.
Faux brick lined the kitchen walls, giving it a shabby cottage feel, and the low ceiling made the space seem closed
in and dark. Despite the dated interior, I saw possibility.
If you stripped everything away and opened up the ceiling, a simple floor plan was revealed. I knew I would need
a contractor to take a look before I finalized an offer, but
something about this little house told me it held great
potential. I loved the location, tucked up into the hills. I
loved how quiet it seemed. I made my way around the

house, mentally taking inventory of all the work that needed to be done.

"I think I like this one," I said to Josh.

"Really?" he questioned, surprised.

"Yeah," I said, "if you bust out the ceiling and open it up a bit, it could be really nice."

He looked around, still unsure but trying to see what I saw.

"Okay," he finally said. "Think about it a little tonight, and then if you still like it, let's talk tomorrow about putting in an offer."

That night I called Christine and described the little broken-down house. She loved the idea and thought it would be an ideal project for me. I called a contractor to take a look the next day and got the all clear. I put in an offer, and after a few negotiations, the house up in the hills was mine.

When I'd moved from New York, I had kept my old job for ESPN, working out of a small production office. The day the deal closed, Josh came by my office to drop off the keys to my new house. I took the short trip up the twisty canyon after work and stood hesitantly outside the front door before finally opening it and walking inside. It was starting to get dark, and as I walked around, my footsteps echoed off the hardwood floors. Suddenly I wasn't sure about this. I wanted to be excited about my new life, or the one I was working toward. But all I felt standing in the entry of my new house was alone.

It was interesting to me how, three years after Pat had died, the happy things in life made me the saddest. The moments when something really good or exciting happened, like when I got the job for ESPN or learned that old friends were getting married, or even when mundane stuff happened, like when I found a great new restaurant, I still turned to share it with Pat and felt the loss of him quickly and severely. In an instant, my emotions would switch from cheerful to devastated as I realized the one person I wanted to share any happy moment with was gone.

Also, I knew I had a tedious and probably painful task ahead of me. When I'd left our little cottage in Washington, I'd put everything Pat and I owned in storage. Now that I was staying put for a while, the time had come to go through it all, so I booked a flight to Seattle and a hotel room for one night. I didn't tell anyone from my old job that I'd be in town, and didn't tell anyone other than Christine that I'd even be gone from Los Angeles.

Flying in, watching the many waterways, islands, peninsulas, and archipelagos that fit together like a three-dimensional puzzle, felt strange. Though I'd loved the scenery in the Northwest, loved many of the people I'd met there, what I wanted was to get to the storage unit, get my stuff done, and get out. This was a trip of necessity, not pleasure. I landed at Sea-Tac Airport and made my way to the rental cars, remembering how I'd gotten a flat tire in the Sea-Tac garage late one night, when Pat had been deployed to Iraq. I'd sat in my car for a minute, recognizing that my life as a military wife meant taking care of this sort of thing by myself. And in the end, it felt empowering not to have to call anyone besides AAA to come save me.

———

When Pat and I lived in Arizona together, we went about decorating our home in a collaborative way. Pat was opinionated about everything in life, and décor was no different. Rule one was that it shouldn't be too feminine. Rule two was that it couldn't be showy. I've always liked things to be a certain style; I feel it's an expression of who you are. But when I was in my early twenties, I was more self-conscious about my spending, because of Pat's aversion to it. Though Pat's childhood had an abundance of love and laughter, money was often tight, and there wasn't much room for material objects. This made him one of the most thoughtful and creative gift givers I've ever met, and gave him an appreciation for the little things. We bought very simple furniture for our house in Phoenix and kept the whole place understated.

Overall, when we talked about house stuff—"What do you think of this couch?" "Don't you think a wine rack would look nice in that corner?"—in a lot of ways, it felt like playing house. We were twenty-two, and the whole idea of picking out furniture and paint colors and vacuuming on weekends and mowing the lawn was novel; trips to the hardware store were exciting.

When I'd moved us to Washington while Pat was in basic training, I knew his taste well enough that I made the house reflect both of our likes and dislikes. I like clean, uncluttered spaces, so I tried to be minimalist about what went on the walls and bookshelves. But since Pat liked knickknacks, I reserved some shelf space and grouped his favorite belongings together. A game ball from when Pat was in Little League got pole position on a bookshelf near his books of philosophy, history, and poetry. Other decorations included a framed picture of Tiger, the gigantic tabby cat he'd had as a kid; and a framed picture of Winston Churchill.

During the time I'd lived in the cottage with just Kevin after Pat was gone, we had made no changes to our environment. We were trying to live in some weird alternative world where Pat was still alive. I moved among Pat's things but never touched them, and the house looked just as he'd left it. Just in case he came back, I'd reasoned at the time. He would need his things. He would need his socks and the frayed T-shirts worn in just the right places. I couldn't get rid of them or even stomach putting them away. When an old friend of ours, Jim, came to visit soon before I left for New York, I could tell he was taken aback when he entered the house. Pictures of Pat and signs of his presence were everywhere, from his shoes still casually thrown in the corner of the room, to his coats in the closet, to his books and decorative hiking boot on the shelves. The only sign of his death was a huge picture that hung over the fireplace, of him sitting in a tree, gun in hand, taken a few days before he had been killed.

"Hey, Marie, I know I'm only here for the afternoon, but why don't I come back and help you go through some of this stuff?" Jim said after looking around, then added tactfully, "It looks like a lot of work."

"Oh, thanks," I said, "but that's okay—it shouldn't be too bad." The truth was the comment made me feel physically assaulted. I wanted to do it alone. At that time, I felt like everything about Pat's life had become public, and I didn't want anyone—no matter how good a friend or how pure his intentions—touching the objects of our lives together. It would have felt like he was trespassing.

Kevin moved out before I did. I blocked out the weekend before I moved to New York, and got boxes, tape, and packing material, and tried to prepare myself emotionally for what I had to do. I approached it gently, telling myself that I only had to go through the top drawer in the dresser. I opened it slowly and peeked in at the rows of socks and undershirts. Brown military-issued versions were shoved next to his civilian wear. His military gear had never seemed like him, and stood out in contrast to his often colorful wardrobe choices. Still, I carefully pulled out each pair of brown cotton socks, folded them together, and placed them in a box for safekeeping. I worked slowly for several hours, emptying drawers into boxes, sealing them up, and labeling their contents. Then I went out onto the porch, sat in the sun, and watched the boats float over the water, wondering about the people on board and the lives they lived. For three days, I sorted, folded, and packed away, never throwing out a thing. Each night I watched the sunset over the narrows. On the fourth day, a moving truck came, taking most of our belongings to storage.

I moved to New York with a couple of suitcases only. I wasn't sure how long I would be in Manhattan, and I told myself it was less expensive to buy a few things to furnish my tiny apartment than to move everything across the country. I became very good at playing tricks with myself so that I could pretend that things were not as they were. In reality, I couldn't bear the thought of seeing the things we'd shared—the things we'd had for years in our homes in Phoenix and then in Washington—crammed into a tiny apartment in the city. So other than my clothes, everything sat in storage. I'd thought of it as locking this life up, tucking it away to be pulled out at another time.

Now, two years later, I collected my rental car and drove out to the nondescript storage facility. The 9 x 10–foot room was just as I'd left it—crammed floor to ceiling with boxes, chairs, and tables. The furniture was all piled at the back of the unit, so I examined the boxes in front first. While I habitually throw everything away and am not very sentimental, Pat was. He kept every nice note he'd received from a coach or fan, every report card, every jersey and game ball, every trinket his mom had given him over the years. If they'd been mine, I would have tossed them long ago. I wasn't going to display all this stuff at the new house, but I didn't have the heart to throw them away when they'd meant so much to Pat. I put those boxes aside to mail to California, no doubt to sit in my garage for a while. I figured one day I'd be ready to let them go.

Framed photographs came next. I'd taken a lot to New York, but dozens more sat in boxes. Photos of our high school crowd, of celebrating after ASU beat Cal to go to the Rose Bowl, of Thanksgiving in Arizona, of holidays in Tahoe, of our snow-covered yard in University Place after a storm that left us housebound, of Pat in a child-sized Halloween costume he'd bought at a grocery store on the way to a party. As with my wedding ring, there was no rule book for what to do with these snapshots.

When I'd lived in New York, I'd become friends with a 9/11 widower. He'd remarried, and I was hanging out at his house one day and noticed he had pictures of his late wife up everywhere. I can't say exactly why, but it felt strange to me. The photos seemed dated, as I knew photos of Pat soon would. Pat would forever be twenty-seven, frozen in time, while I was growing older every day. But if I didn't have photos up, wouldn't people who came to my house think that was strange? If I had too many photos up, would people think *that* was strange? So much significance was attached to these small prints, and in the end, as I sat in the concrete storage facility, contemplating the problem, I was just tired of it all. Pat was much more than these photos. Pat was part of my daily thoughts and decisions, whether I had his image up on the wall or not. He was a part of me, like my arm. I didn't need to look down at it to know it was there; it just *was*. I'd ship those boxes to California, I decided, but I wouldn't put all the pictures up at my new house.

Pat's clothes were easier to deal with, as I no longer expected him to come home looking to put them back on. The boxes were neatly labeled, and I knew once I got them home to L.A., I could search through them and make sure there wasn't a favorite sweatshirt or hat I'd want to hold on to. Finally I came to the furniture—the Pottery Barn couch, the cottagey throw pillows and comforters. Before coming up here, I'd thought maybe some of the furniture could be used in my new house, but as I examined the dark brown chairs, beige couch, and rust-colored throw pillows, I realized I was looking at an old life. My style had changed; the house was different; the scenery was different. I was different.

—

Back in Los Angeles, I went to the bookstore and bought every home magazine available. I pored over the pages, trying to figure out what I wanted my new house to look like. In the end I kept things pretty simple: dark wood floors, white walls, white marble countertops with subtle gray veins running through them. This house was like many things in my life now, gutted to the essence. My external space became a reflection of my internal space. Only the essentials were left.

Once the construction was done and I was finally able to sleep in the house, I started getting excited about making it a home. Now that I had 1,600 square feet to do whatever I wanted with, it was kind of exhilarating. I wanted it to be calm and comfortable, and even a bit girly. I didn't have to take anyone else's taste into consideration when picking paint colors or bedding, and I found some joy in knowing I could do whatever I wanted. I became a little obsessed with wallpaper and found a beautiful print with large flowers that wound up the walls of my bedroom. It was certainly more feminine than I would have picked in the past, but I loved it. I ended up with a mostly neutral palette of soft grays, beige, and white, but little splashes of color appeared in turquoise vases, lilac pillows, and pink throws.

The exterior received a face-lift, too, with a fresh coat of light gray paint and white trim, keeping with the simple neutral palette. For the front door, I wanted a little color and settled on a sunny shade of yellow that made me smile every time I came home. I planted a small cutting garden of hydrangeas and roses in the front courtyard so I could always have fresh flowers in the house, and nurtured the avocado tree that was already there. As I slowly brought the house back to life, I felt life coming back to me as well.

While I was trying to be a bit more social in Los Angeles, I still relished time alone, and the little house felt like the perfect place to regroup after too much time traveling for work or being around people. As soon as I started the climb up the hills and turned onto my little street, I felt better. Up here it was quiet; I could hear birds in the middle of the day and coyotes at night. I could find the solitude I still craved when I felt like I needed to think.

Shortly after moving in, I had a long day at work, dealing with a variety of mundane problems—another appearance cancellation, another agent fretting about the perception of his client appearing on an ESPN show. I wound my way up the canyon to my new little house, feeling the stress dissipate as my car climbed up the hill. I pulled into the drive and noticed a bottle of wine and a note. I looked around, wondering who had left the gift, and ripped open the note.

Welcome to the neighborhood, it read. *You've chosen a truly magical place.* It was signed by the neighbors to my left.

I hope so. I smiled to myself. *I could use a little magic.*

———

One of the biggest selling points of moving to Southern California was the proximity of some of my dearest friends from high school: Ben, Jamie, and Brandon. Ben and Pat had known each other since kindergarten, and Ben and I had become fast friends when we'd met at Leland High. Jamie—now Ben's wife—was a year younger than us. She and I had been cheerleaders together in high school, and I'd always appreciated her carefree spirit. Brandon was Ben's younger brother. He was Kevin's age, and the two of them were close friends, so the whole group just meshed together.

Jamie had gone to ASU with Pat, and whenever she'd see him on campus, she'd run up and jump on him. She was the only person who could get away with that, as she was like a little sister to him. Ben and Jamie bought a place in Lake Tahoe, and Pat and I would spend vacations there along with other close friends, skiing in the winter and hanging out on the lake in the summer. We'd drink beer and have dance parties in the kitchen in the evenings, and felt completely at ease with one another. A lot of times with couple friends, the men might be friends or the women might be friends, but it's harder to find a fit where all are equally friends. That's what we had with Ben and Jamie and, extending it, with Brandon and Kevin.

While we had been close for a long time, the past couple of years since Pat had died had brought us even closer. It was still amazing to me how things shook out after Pat's death. Some of the friends I thought would be of comfort weren't, and those relationships slowly faded away. Meanwhile, other relationships strengthened amid the turmoil, and Ben, Jamie, and Brandon quickly became like family. Pat had a lot of friends who I wasn't as close with, who reached out to me after he died. I loved them for the gesture, but I also knew they were doing it for him and didn't really know me. And then I had friends reach out to me who had been in my life since childhood, but who hadn't known Pat. But Ben, Jamie, and Brandon knew and loved us both. When Ben and Jamie had a baby less than a year after Pat died, Ben felt a deep ache of missing Pat and not being able to share the joy of having his first child with his friend. He could relate to what I was going through like no other friend could.

When I moved to Los Angeles, we often got together for dinner on Sundays. I loved having a place to go where I could feel at home, loved being with people who knew and understood me and were able to accept the bad with the good. There were no pretenses; I could be angry or sad. I could sit on Ben and Jamie's couch and eat pizza and watch television all day without feeling like I was putting them out. But mostly, time with them calmed me down, helped me feel centered and loved. When the whirlwind of life seemed too much, they helped bring everything into perspective and helped me realize how important relationships were in my life. It was important to me to feel connected to other people and know that I wasn't alone in the world.

One Sunday I picked up some wine and drove out

to Ben and Jamie's. I'd been looking forward to dinner all week. After a long slog at work, I just wanted to relax with old friends and enjoy the warm summer night. ESPN had put on an event in Los Angeles that week, and as I had been setting things up and fielding questions left and right, an irate sports agent had come over to me and started yelling about the size of his client's hotel room. Though I knew better than to take it personally, the encounter was still with me.

"Rough week?" Jamie asked when I walked in.

"How can you tell?"

"*Two* bottles of wine," she said.

"Just a crazy month at work," I said. But as I settled in, and as we all sat down for dinner by the pool, we started talking more about my job. "I don't think this is what I want to do anymore," I said, surprising myself. I told them about the experience of getting yelled at by the agent. Not that it was a new occurrence, exactly, but I was sick of it. "You wouldn't believe these expos set up for the athletes." I described the scene before the show: We'd had a hotel suite chock-full of expensive watches, jackets, hats, and bags for the celebrities to pick from. The manufacturers reasoned that if so-and-so was photographed for *People* magazine wearing their brand of jacket or purse, well, then, the rest of the world would want it, too. Part of my job was to make sure the celebrities were exposed to all the merchandise. "See how I contribute to society?" I laughed. "I help make kids everywhere want a Rolex."

"That's crazy," Ben said, stuck on the image of hotel rooms packed with swag. "Who lives like that?"

"And how can I?" asked Brandon. "Seriously, Marie—can you hook me up?"

"I'll see what I can do." I smiled. "I don't know...it's not *all* bad. Sometimes we do cool, meaningful stuff, and Maura's great. And I don't have any idea what I'd do next. It's all well and good to want what you do to matter, but it's not like you just snap your fingers and it happens."

"Of course it doesn't," said Jamie, "because you're working all the time. You need to take some time off, get away, think about some of this stuff."

"Yeah, maybe," I said, and tried to turn the conversation away from me. But I kept thinking about what Jamie had said. Of course, she also thought I should get married eight or nine more times, because falling in love is fun, she reasoned, and weddings are fun. Though I took her free-spirited advice with a grain of salt, it *had* been a long time since I'd traveled for anything other than work. I hadn't left the country since Pat had died. Maybe I should. It would be great to get away, see something new, and just break away from my routine for a while. The uncertainty of exploring a new city had always excited me, and I realized I missed the adventure of it all.

I'm both a planner and impulsive. After the evening's dinner, I went with my latter tendencies. I told Maura I was leaving ESPN, but didn't have a plan for what I would do next. Another media job materialized, but I wasn't sure I wanted it. While I closed things out at ESPN, I surveyed my friends as traveling companions. Most of them were married or had kids or jobs that were hard to leave, so I decided I'd just go alone. I refused to let the "single" part stop me.

I had a few cities on my short list of places I wanted to visit, and told my childhood friend Erin that Buenos Aires was one of the top three contenders. "Marie!" Erin practically shouted. "You know Juan still lives there, right?" Juan had been an exchange student at our high school. He'd become friends with both me and Pat and had gone to prom with our group of friends. After the year ended and Juan went back to Argentina, Erin kept in touch with him. I sent him an email, not really expecting a response, but a few short days later I heard back from him. He wrote that he was excited to show me around his city, and when could I come? It was just the push I needed, and I booked my flight.

On the night of my thirty-first birthday, I boarded a plane to Buenos Aires, looking for a little adventure, some introspection, and perspective on what I should do with my life. I landed at night, tired from the travel and the time change. I collected my luggage and clambered into a taxi, and as we drove through the lights of the unfamiliar city, I had a moment of fear. Some concerned people in my life had been uncertain about the Argentina trip, had told me they weren't sure it was a good idea for a woman to be traveling alone in a South American country. Though I had brushed the comments off, they came back to me. The fact was that I was in a big city, in a big country, in a big world, and I was by myself. *No one knows where I am*, I thought. I'd planned the trip so quickly that I hadn't told anyone what my itinerary was or where I was staying. Something could happen to me, and no one would know where to look. Through my mind ran countless movie trailers of the woman who disappears while traveling, and the brave sister who takes off to find her. When I got to my hotel, I sent Christine an email and told her the basics of where I was and planned to be. Then I thought about Pat, and how ridiculous he would think my train of thought. He loved nothing more than an adventure and would never have let fear stand in his way. Neither would I. There was so much to be afraid of in life, and I was tired of it.

That was the last time I felt fear or doubt in Argentina.

After sleeping my first morning away, I got dressed and wandered around the streets near my hotel, taking it all in. Buenos Aires is a city full of juxtapositions, a mix of old world and modern, with as many high-end, slick neighborhoods as downtrodden areas. Its rocky economic past was still evident around the city, but the lively spirit of its people emanated from even the most dilapidated streets.

My hotel was situated in Recoleta, a short walk to a famous cemetery full of elaborate marble mausoleums. Past the cemetery was an open-air flea market with stalls stretching for miles. There were thousands of leather goods for sale, endless jewelry, and more food to sample than you could try in a year. It was a feast for the senses. I walked aimlessly, still a little jet-lagged from the long flight. I walked over to one vendor selling leather bags and belts, and my eye caught a pair of funny leather sandals that reminded me of a pair Pat used to own. They weren't full-on gladiator sandals, with leather straps going up the leg, but they were pretty close. While everyone around him had worn Tevas and Birkenstocks, there was Pat with his handmade leather shoes from some little shop in Arizona. He'd worn them proudly until they broke. The memory didn't make me sad, which surprised me.

"You like them?" asked the vendor.

"Yes, very much," I said, and smiled at him. I ran my fingers over the sandals for sale, feeling the cool leather and intricate braiding. *Pat would love it here*, I thought.

Pat had been so much fun to travel with. While I had the travel bug before he did, and had been the instigator and planner of our first long trip to Europe when we lived in Arizona, Pat quickly caught the bug, too. People go one of two ways when traveling: They either are afraid of a new situation, or they're curious. And he was always curious. In fact, Pat was the most curious person I'd ever known, and going out of the country with a curious person is like going to Disneyland with a five-year-old. It was a delicious display of sheer energy and enthusiasm.

"What do you suppose that's all about?" he'd ask when we'd come across a random statue in France, or a half-crumbled wall in Rome. He'd ask this dozens of times a day as we meandered our way through big cities and tiny villages. And he wanted to taste *everything*; he was on a quest to find the best beer in Germany, the most delicious croissants in France, the thickest Guinness in Ireland.

He also wanted to talk to *everyone*. While I always felt more comfortable blending in, staying off the radar, he was outgoing. At home, he'd become friends with the UPS guy, the baristas at the café down the street, and nearly every neighbor or teammate he ever had. When traveling, he was no different. He chatted with everyone from the people in the ticket line ahead of us at the Louvre to the Irish fisherman sitting next to us at a pub. We took a long train ride through Germany, and we'd barely settled into our seats before Pat engaged the German couple sitting across the aisle from us.

"Do you speak English?" he asked.

"Yes, a bit," the husband said.

They chitchatted for a minute about where we each were headed. Before long, Pat asked, "So what was it like before the wall came down?" and followed it up with a lengthy discussion about East and West Berlin.

People seldom minded his questions; he was open and earnest, and strangers saw that right away. The couple were impressed with his knowledge of German history and politics, and they talked easily for hours. At first, I sat behind my book, listening. Gradually I put it down and became more active in the conversation myself. I knew Pat would record all of it in his journal later that night. He wanted to process and remember everything he was soaking in.

———

My first few days in Buenos Aires, I felt more free and alive than I had in a while. Discovering the sights and sounds of a new place made me realize how my surroundings at home often fell into a hazy background I paid little attention to. For instance, I had already become so used to the little birds that filled the trees outside my house that I barely noticed them anymore; but here in the streets of Buenos Aires, everything came at me full force. I took a step back just to let it all sink in, vowing to take the same approach to my home when I returned.

To get myself in the traveling mood, I had brought along an anthology of travel essays. Pico Iyer had written an introduction to it that I loved. He had noted that "travel...guides us toward a better balance of wisdom and compassion—of seeing the world clearly, and yet feeling it truly. For seeing without feeling can obviously be uncaring; while feeling without seeing can be blind." Another favorite line I'd underlined was "That is why many of us travel not in search of answers, but in search of better questions."

As I wandered the cobblestone streets, Iyer in my head, decisions seemed much simpler. Gone was the anxiety over what to do with my life. To anyone observing my recent actions, it might have looked like I didn't know which way was up. "She moved *again*? She left her job and took off for South America? Someone help that girl!" But that was just perception; that wasn't reality. Somehow, here, now that I'd taken a step away, my life became clearer. I knew I didn't want to take a job I didn't feel passionate about. I knew my work had to contribute to some greater good. I also knew I'd find my way to it. I had some money saved up, so I didn't need to worry about finding something immediately. And I could craft my world into what I wanted it to be.

After the initial shock wore off, I realized that traveling alone could be very freeing. I could wander and decide for myself, with no one else's opinions or thoughts to consider. I sometimes set out for a destination and then changed my course along the way. Or I arrived at my destination only to realize I wasn't really interested in looking at modern art anymore but would rather find a café and people-watch the afternoon away. In the evenings, I returned to my modest, but comfortable hotel.

I remembered how Pat and I had tromped through Europe on our shoestring budget years before. I wouldn't have had it any other way; I loved keeping our accommodations simple, immersing ourselves in the world around our hotel's walls. Still, now I appreciated having a comfortable place to stay and a soft bed to sleep on.

Once when Pat and I had driven up the West Coast en route to Vancouver, Canada, we'd spent one night sleeping in the back of his Jeep. What's more, Pat had been training for a triathlon at the time and didn't want his bike to get wet from the weather. So even though he'd played with the NFL two seasons by then and was making decent money, we shared the back of his car with his bike for a cramped and sleepless night. I had wanted to be a good sport, so I'd stretched out as best I could, mindful of not getting my hair stuck in his bike chain. It was a memory, for sure, but I think now I would have suggested—maybe even insisted—we spring the fifty dollars and stay at the motel down the road.

———

In the two short weeks between when I'd booked my flight and when I'd left for Argentina, I'd amassed from friends a list of acquaintances in Buenos Aires. My old self—never wanting to put people out and always a little shy and uncomfortable around people I didn't know— never would have reached out to a stranger. This time, though, I figured, why not? In the time since Pat had died, I had been in a variety of uncomfortable, public situations; there had been the hearings, of course, but there'd also been events like standing before thousands live and god knows how many on television when the Cardinals retired his jersey. But the one good thing that had come from all of it was I had finally shed the last of my shy demeanor. Somehow in the midst of all the chaos, I'd become more comfortable with myself and more willing to seek out new people and new experiences. Perhaps it was practice, or perhaps it was the realization of how short life can be.

One friend-of-a-friend living in Buenos Aires was a Swedish woman named Sigried. Over a year before, she'd taken a trip down there, fallen in love with the tango, and decided to stay and learn to dance. I loved the romantic notion of it all and was excited to meet up. After emailing back and forth, we decided to meet at a little bar in her neighborhood. I was eager to find out more about her decision to leave her life in Sweden and move to Buenos Aires. Though I'd been in town only three short days, I could already see the allure of the city and was fantasizing about moving myself. I couldn't imagine really doing it, but maybe after seeing Sigried, I'd feel differently.

I arrived at the bar a few minutes late and found a tall, thin girl, with long blonde hair almost to her waist, waiting outside. I hesitated as I walked up, thinking it might not be her, but then again, her hair and stature made her stand out from the Argentinians milling around her.

"Sigried?" I asked.

"Yes." She smiled. "You must be Marie. So nice to meet you."

I guessed that she was a little older than me, but she looked youthful in her fitted, leotard-like top and flowing skirt. She was going to dance class after our drink and was dressed accordingly. I followed her into the bar and out to the back patio, where the buzz of conversation from the other patrons livened up the space. It was springtime in Buenos Aires, but not too hot yet, and the air on the patio felt refreshing. We each ordered a glass of Malbec and chatted easily for over an hour. Sigried had worked in a fairly demanding job as a journalist in Sweden when on a whim she had decided to take a sabbatical and go to Argentina. Like me, she had needed a break from the routine of her life and had been urged on by a feeling that there must be something more than the daily grind of her job back home. She had instantly fallen in love with Buenos Aires, and tango in particular, and had spent her monthlong sabbatical dancing her days and nights away. Before her time in the city was over, she had decided to move and had found a small house to rent. She went back to Sweden to quit her job and gather her things, then returned to Argentina to live. She now worked as a freelance writer for an American website, reporting mostly on women's issues in South America. The dollar went pretty far in Argentina, and Sigried was able to maintain a nice lifestyle that left her plenty of time to dance.

Sigried made it all seem simple and perfect, and I wondered if I could ever do the same thing. There had been many times after Pat's death when I had thought about leaving everything behind, packing a small bag and traveling the world, but something stopped me. I had responsibilities at home, the first few years the investigations into his death were always looming, and now even though I wasn't running the daily operations at the Pat Tillman Foundation, I did feel it was important for me to oversee its activities and stay involved. It didn't seem right to leave.

After we finished our drinks, we said our good-byes and Sigried told me a couple of places to try out tango. I walked back to my hotel, thinking about how she had just taken the leap and left her old life behind. I wondered if she would stay, or if, in time, she would feel the pull of her friends and family back home.

Juan and I arranged to meet in the lobby of my hotel. I hadn't seen him since we had graduated from high school nearly fifteen years before, but despite his receding hairline and slightly hunched frame, I recognized him right away. He still had the same look of mischief in his blue eyes and the adorable smile, which spread across his face when I stood up to greet him. So much time had passed, and it wasn't clear how to summarize all that had happened. We hugged and sat down in the lobby sitting area, talking about where all our mutual friends had ended up—who had three kids already, who lived where. At one point he leaned in and made direct eye contact with me. "So how are you?" I'd gotten used to this question by then, and the variety of ways I might answer it.

"I'm still dealing with things," I said, "but I'm doing okay."

"Come, then," he said, "let me show you my city." I had my own private tour guide in Juan. He shared all of his city's history, took me to known tourist spots, like the Plaza de Mayo and Casa Rosada, and off the beaten path to a little café where his parents used to go before he was born. We spent the day seeing every corner of the city, and ended up at an outdoor café in Palermo Soho. I told him all about the Swedish tango dancer and how I was obsessed now with finding a place to take tango while I was there.

"Ah, then we must go dance," he said. "I will pick you up tomorrow night. There is a perfect local place you must see."

"Really?"

"Hm," he said. "You must see the real tango. Most tourists go to see a tango show, but the shows are all in the traditional style."

"What do you mean? It's different now?"

"Yes, very. It used to be a lower-class thing, done in a traditional way," he said, adopting his tour guide voice, "but now it's changed. Young people love it now, and have changed its reputation. They changed the dance a bit, too. You'll see."

The nightlife in Argentina doesn't begin until well after my usual bedtime, but I'd found myself enjoying the late nights there and not worrying about sleeping half the day away. Juan picked me up at my hotel around eleven-thirty the next night and we took a taxi to San Telmo. We stopped in front of a nondescript building and Juan paid the taxi driver as I wondered if this was the right address. I hadn't been expecting a big glitzy club, necessarily, but this was just a small community center with lessons upstairs and tango dancing downstairs. As far as I could tell, I was the only tourist around.

"Let's watch a little first," said Juan. We found seats at a small table not too far from the dance floor, and I was mesmerized. Men, women, and children of all ages crowded the floor, moving in unison through what looked like very elaborate routines. Some couples put their own spin on the dance and were quite theatrical, while others easily, casually moved around, enjoying the music and their partners. I was struck by the feeling of family and community in this room. We had nothing like it back home. It wasn't a bar or a club with loud music and half-drunk teenagers, but a place for everyone in the community to come together and enjoy themselves. Babies sat perched on grandmothers' knees while their parents twirled around next to teenage couples clearly on dates. After almost an hour of watching, Juan and I went upstairs to take a beginners' class. He had done a little tango over the years and was a patient partner as I stumbled over myself. The moves were even harder than they'd looked when I'd been an observer downstairs. As a kid, I had taken years of dance lessons, and eventually it all came together and I started to feel less awkward. Regardless of how I looked, it was fun. I let myself enjoy the music and the time spent dancing with my old friend.

And as I danced through the early morning hours, in a community center in the middle of Buenos Aires, I thought about how happy Pat would be if he could see me.

CHAPTER NINE

Thanksgiving fell right after the trip to Argentina, and I hoped the travel high would see me through what was always a difficult holiday. I went home to the Bay Area and spent my first night visiting with Christine and Alex. We sat around their living room after they put their boys to bed, drinking coffee and talking about the holiday and the weeks ahead. Alex had left his post as director of the Pat Tillman Foundation not long before, crossing back over to the for-profit sector. Though we'd hired a replacement, we were concerned that she wasn't working out.

"I think we need to start searching again," Alex said, frowning. No doubt he was trying to figure where he'd find the time for interviews among the responsibilities of his new job and his young kids.

"I'm not working right now," I said, surprising myself. "I can do the job for a while."

Christine and Alex were quiet a minute, and so was I. Obviously, it made sense, and we all realized that. I had the time. And I'd been involved in the foundation from the beginning.

But there was another side. I'd avoided being the public face of the foundation in the years since we'd started it for good reasons. Though I was always involved behind the scenes, feeling great responsibility to use the money we'd been given in an honorable and intelligent manner, mine was very much a hidden role. What public appearances I *had* done had left me feeling horrible. One of them was an event at the Pro Football Hall of Fame not long after Pat died. The organization was inducting several new members, and they wanted to make a special presentation for Pat. I'd let them use his Class A uniform and his Cardinals uniform, which they'd encased in a glass exhibit in a section of the museum that told a bit of his story. The Hall of Fame group flew Alex and me out and took very good care of us for the duration of our stay. They were sweet, and the honor would have meant a lot to Pat.

On the day of the presentation, I waited backstage as the former players who were being inducted milled about. One came up to me and said, "Thank you so much for your sacrifice." I know military families hear this all the time, and they do indeed sacrifice, but it seemed like an odd statement. I thanked him, but what I wanted to say was "I didn't want this sacrifice. I didn't make a choice to lose my husband this way, and if I could, I would take him back in a second, sacrifice be damned." It was a two-second encounter, but it left me shaken. Only minutes later, I was called onto the stage to be presented with a commemorative plaque. I stepped out into the sunlight, and thousands of people in the crowd got on their feet. It was bizarre; I hadn't done anything, and yet everyone was applauding, for minutes on end, while I stood there awkwardly, wanting badly just to run offstage.

Pat used to talk all the time about the difference between being rewarded for something you worked hard for and being rewarded for something that came easily. One reason he always lived simply, even after he was making good money as an NFL player, was that it didn't make sense to him that he was disproportionately compensated for something he loved to do. Yes, he worked hard, as most professional athletes do, but lots of people worked just as hard for far less. His uncle Mike had worked as a mechanic for an airline all his life, yet his compensation was nothing compared to Pat's. It hadn't seemed fair to Pat then, and this outpouring of recognition didn't seem right to me now. I hated being in that spotlight for as long as it took people to take their seats so I could say a brief "On behalf of Pat's family, thank you."

People had all these feelings about Pat that needed to

go somewhere, and I was a living representation of him. But I wasn't the one who had gone to Iraq, who had gone to Afghanistan. All I'd done was step out on a stage when someone told me it was time.

From that event onward, I ducked the spotlight as much as I could. I needed to move on with my life, and running a foundation with Pat's name attached would be like inviting people to put whatever they felt about Pat onto me. And at the same time, the investigations were in full swing, and it would have been impossible to attend foundation functions and not get questions about how I felt about the fratricide, questions I didn't care to answer.

Alex knew all this and understood. Christine knew it, too. And yet, things had changed. Years had passed since that Hall of Fame presentation. The fratricide investigation was behind us. Now I was less raw. Now I just might be ready.

"I think you'd do a great job," Alex said, choosing his words carefully. "But only if you think it's the right time for you to do it."

"I agree," said Christine. "You should think about it a bit. Let's keep talking about it. Take a few days and see how it sits."

"Right," Alex agreed. "There's no huge rush. We don't need to figure this out tonight."

We finished our coffee, and I drove back to my parents' house. I lay in bed awake for a long time, thinking about how quickly I'd suggested I take over, and how right it had felt once the words were out of my mouth. I didn't need any more time to make this decision. I'd been in the process of making it for years.

———

When Pat and I lived in University Place, we often took the same walk. We parked at the top of a bluff and walked down a steep stairway to the beach. Beaches in the Northwest tend to be rocky, so it was a different feeling than going to our Santa Cruz spot, but we loved it. We could always count on seeing dogs dash into the water after salty sticks and seagulls coasting on the winds from ferry boats, and sometimes we'd spot a family of sea lions. On one occasion, we took our walk and were about to climb back up the steps when we saw an old fisherman struggling with a line on his boat.

"Go ahead and go back to the car," Pat said. "I'll be there in a minute."

He turned and approached the fisherman, and before I reached the first step, he'd clambered aboard the man's boat and was helping him. I stopped halfway up the steps to watch. The fisherman was small; Pat towered over him. Though I wasn't close enough to hear what they were saying, it was clear they were laughing and the old man was really happy to have the help. I stood still, watching, and tears filled my eyes.

Pat was always doing things, large and small, to help

other people. No matter what he was doing, or how absorbed he was in what he needed to get done on a given day, he'd always stop; he'd always help the fisherman. I constantly imagined what the world would be like if everyone was like Pat.

Sometimes—and this is hard to describe in words—when Pat performed an act of kindness, something about him just broke my heart, and I almost couldn't look at him. He had this very innocent quality, this optimism about the world. Children have it, but they get older and this eagerness is often replaced with cynicism. That Pat *was* older, knew the way the world really worked, and yet held on to this idealism made him *more* special. When things didn't play out the way he expected them to—like his early time in the military—it hurt me all the more, because his intentions were pure. I wanted badly for the world to meet him at his level.

I don't know where this part of Pat's personality came from, exactly. I've talked to his mom about it, and she says he was always like that, from the time he was a kid. Sometimes I think some people are just different and have something inside them that's really special, but no one knows why that is or where it comes from. He simply seemed more evolved than your average person, especially after he joined the military. Buddhists would have said he'd lived many lives before, growing wiser and more enlightened with each one. That made some sense to me. Right after he died, Kevin and I used to say that

Pat had evolved so much in the past few years that he evolved straight off the earth. That was the only image that offered me any comfort during that time.

And unless people knew Pat, they didn't get it. They couldn't understand how someone who was intelligent and well read could make the decisions he did, so they put him into a box as another macho guy who wanted to prove something to himself and the world. But it's much more complicated than that. Pat saw the world the way he thought it should be. That it wasn't always that way, well, that was beside the point. He *chose* to see it the way he wanted it to be.

Though by nature I am much more cynical than Pat was, he led me to the periphery of his orbit slowly in our early years together, when we'd talk about current events or just our outlooks on the world. He pulled me in entirely when he decided to enlist. It was the first time I'd ever felt a connection to something greater than me. It was an embrace of a world where people don't just sit around and let events transpire—be it a fisherman's struggle with an anchor, or a horrific act of terrorism— but instead take an active role in making things better.

After Pat died, it was hard for me to find my way back there. First and foremost, my survival instinct told me that I needed to take care of myself, I needed just to get through. But when I was working for ESPN, glimmers of his perspective reappeared. Once, Maura and I went down to New Orleans to prepare for a massive television event: a Monday-night football game, the first football game played in New Orleans since Hurricane Katrina. We arrived the Sunday before the game and asked a cab to take us directly to the stadium. Our driver had recently returned to the city, but a lot of his friends and relatives were not coming back or were missing entirely. He remarked that the cleaned-up area around the stadium did not present a clear picture of the still-devastated city.

At the stadium, I went onto the field to meet with one of the producers of the halftime show. The movable stage was set up in the middle of the field, and U2 and Green Day soon came out for sound checks and to play a few songs.

I sat down on the turf to watch. Though I'd been moved by U2 when I'd seen them perform at Madison Square Garden that night with Carolyn, this was much more intimate. The bands were there to bring attention to the city's urgent needs and to help promote Music Rising, an organization providing relief to New Orleans musicians. Sitting there, watching these great musicians interact with one another, without the glare and the cheers, I realized how they had chosen to use their power to help others. They recognized their ability to harness the energy of their fans and focus it toward a greater good. Somewhere in their journey, their eyes had been opened, and they couldn't ignore the needs they saw. There was somehow a tremendous sense of human connection in all this.

In our times, we have amazing new ways of connecting with each other and doing great things. Where the spotlight moves can determine who gets helped, what gets solved, how the world will change. As I sat there watching and listening to these real people preparing to move history a little, I started to find my way back to the world Pat had introduced me to. I wanted to help this grand connection in some way; small would be fine, but I wanted to contribute in some way. Here was something big enough to be worth a life.

Somewhere in between the trip to New Orleans and the trip to Argentina, in ways slow and subtle, it had also dawned on me that while Pat's life had been cut short, mine could be quite long. My grandmother was in her nineties. I might have a long life to live, and there was no point in not making the best of it somehow. Why not try to have some impact? Why not have a life that makes a difference for people? And here I had a tool to do that already at my disposal: a foundation, with a solid board made up of family and friends, and with a message that was as close to my heart as it could get. Just as I could now unpack Pat's socks and shirts, and recall details of our life together without becoming too sad, perhaps I could also embrace his message of altruism without being swept away by the public obsession with his story.

———

I knocked quietly on the bright yellow Dutch door but turned the doorknob and walked in before getting a response. Dannie's door was always open. Inside, scattered around the little kitchen, sat most of the family, home for Thanksgiving: Kevin; his new girlfriend, Kandi; Richard; Pat's uncle Mike; and Dannie. Gram, Dannie and Mike's mom, was in her usual spot on the couch, tucked in a blanket. The dining room table was set for the meal. I had spent many holidays before sitting at that very table, enjoying the fat turkey and lively conversation. This year I had eaten an early dinner at my parents' house, but wanted to stop over at Dannie's and say hi. My trips home were more and more seldom, and I hadn't seen everyone in quite a few months.

"Hi, Marie!" Dannie greeted me warmly, coming over at once to give me a hug. "Here's the world traveler. How was Argentina?"

"It was nice," I said. "How have you been? Dinner looks delicious—I'm sorry that I've already eaten."

"Oh, by the time we sit down, you'll be ready for another bite, I bet."

Dannie's tone was lighthearted, and I recognized how hard she was trying. Everyone was. *Let's talk about food! Let's talk about travel! Let's talk about anything other than the person who's missing today.*

I went over to Kevin and gave him an awkward hug.

"How are you?" he asked. "How's your family doing?" Our eyes met for a brief second before he looked away.

"They're good," I said. "How are you?"

"I'm fine."

"Good." I felt like there should be more, but couldn't think of what to say that was right. I noticed that he'd shaved off his beard, and his head was still neatly shaved, just like it had been for the three years he served in the Army. I remembered how he and Pat used to go down into the basement garage of the house in Washington and cut each other's hair every week. They'd drag a chair from the kitchen down the back stairs and I'd hear their spirited banter over the buzz of the clippers. Then one Sunday night after Pat died, Kevin disappeared into the garage, and I heard the buzz of his clippers. He was down there by himself for a while but eventually came up and asked if I would help him.

I'd walked down to help him, and saw that the hair on the back of his head was an uneven mess of patches. I gently put my hand on his head, then maneuvered the clippers in a sweeping motion to even things out. Then I switched them off, running my hand once more over his head to make sure I didn't miss a spot, that the soft stubble on his head was now uniform. When I was finished, we stood for a second in silence, the loss of Pat all around us.

I had mixed emotions seeing him now. I was happy to see him looking good. The sparkle in his eyes was back, and the loving, gentle way he touched Kandi's arm when he sat down next to her signaled a new softness in his heart. I wondered why distance had grown between us and if it had been my fault. In some ways it was, but we both needed space to process Pat's death on our own, and we were both making progress.

"So, Marie." Dannie jumped in after a silence. "Tell us about the trip. What did you do there?"

"Um, just wandered around," I said. I thought about telling her about Sigried, about Juan and the tango, about the markets and all the incredible food. But I kept self-censoring, not sure how it would all sound to them. I settled on a bland "I spent most of the time in Buenos Aires."

"Oh, that's nice," Dannie said, and everyone nodded.

"Huge turkey," I noted, gesturing to the just-cooked bird resting on the countertop.

It was, everyone agreed.

The first Thanksgiving after Pat died was horrible. I spent the day with his family, all of us trying to enjoy ourselves but heartbreakingly aware of what was missing. The next year was not much better and sent me into a downward spiral that lasted for months. Holidays were still my Achilles' heel, and I anticipated a similar response this season to the forced cheer and hope for the new year; I just prayed the funk didn't last quite so long. I was learning to cope with the waves of grief and was reassured that they were getting shorter and easier to escape as time moved forward. But even three years after Pat died, I found myself thinking about ways to avoid the holidays altogether.

In the first year after Pat's death, I clung to his family and abandoned my own, spending each trip to San Jose with the group that now clustered around the warm kitchen. I felt more comfortable in the midst of their misery, which closely matched my own. But as time went on, things changed. People think death brings everyone together, and it does at first. Then, as time passes and the shock wears off, differences between how people cope are revealed. Each of our relationships to Pat was like a fingerprint unique to each of us, and his loss was felt differently in each of our lives. Husband different from brother, different from son. I tried to understand what they were all feeling, and in some ways I did. But sometimes I didn't recognize the boy they talked about, and as I longed for a connection that wasn't possible, I felt even more alone. Our mutual love of Pat will forever keep us connected, but a distance had developed between all of us.

I stayed for about an hour, tried to engage in the conversation, but I felt strangely self-conscious sharing my new life with them. I knew they wanted me to be happy, just as I wished happiness for all of them, but I was still uncomfortable. They weren't judging me for moving forward with my life; I was judging myself, the sting of guilt—though less pronounced now—still lurking in my mind. While I had once felt more comfortable in the embrace of Pat's childhood home than anywhere else, I now felt like an outsider intruding on their day.

The ripples of loss spread infinitely out. I mourned the loss of Pat, but also the loss of his family. Without him, our relationship to one another changed. We would have to establish another connection—one that didn't as fully encompass loss. I felt hopeful that someday, we would. With Kevin in particular, I knew I'd find my way back to a close relationship. Army life in Washington had bonded Pat, Kevin, and me together in an unexplainable way, and that bond between Kevin and me had further sealed after Pat died. Now we had retreated into our own lives and found different spaces to heal, but I knew that even a little time and distance couldn't change what we had been through. Eventually, we would find our way back to each other.

———

The Pat Tillman Foundation was headquartered in Arizona, but Alex had made it work from his home in San Jose, and I intended to make it work from my home in Los Angeles. I was proud of the progress the foundation had made in its early years. The first thing we'd done was set up an endowment at Arizona State University, known as the Tillman Scholars program. The program selected students with leadership qualities and helped them start social action programs to benefit the community.

But as I threw myself into my new role, reading every book about nonprofits I could find, I wanted to do more. I didn't want the Pat Tillman Foundation to be merely a memorial organization; I didn't think Pat would have felt comfortable with that. I wanted to take it further, to make it something sparked by memory but looking to the future. I met some resistance from people who had been working with the foundation from the beginning, which made sense. It had been running along just fine, honoring Pat and doing some good things along the way. But now that some time had passed and the foundation had found its footing, I felt it could be so much more.

Two of the students in the first class of Tillman Scholars were Marines who had come to ASU after serving in Iraq. Spending time with them, we'd learned about their needs and how little support the military was really able to give them after their service was completed. It occurred to me at the time that someday the military might be an object of focus for the foundation, but the timing wasn't right. That first class of Tillman Scholars came about just as Pat's family and I were in the spotlight as vocal critics of the military, still mired in investigations and hearings.

Now, though, things were different. The investigations, which at one point I had thought would never end, *had* ended. And what was more, though I'd loathed the public attention the hearings brought, one thing that had come out of it was that I had a voice people would listen to about military affairs. I wasn't delusional; I knew I wasn't Bono or anything, capable of moving hearts and minds with every word I spoke. But I did have a very public connection to the military and military issues, and I could use that fact to do some good. If even one person would listen, I felt I had a responsibility to speak up.

The link between the Tillman name and the military was obvious and yet also perplexed people. I admit there was a time when I couldn't go into a supermarket without fearing I'd see someone in uniform and be reminded of what I'd lost. And there was a time when I'd taken all of it personally—the way Pat had been used for propaganda and political purpose. But over time I had realized that while the administration involved in the fratricide cover-up were malicious, they were not malicious toward Pat. It could have been anyone, and they would have done the same thing. Their concern was the end result, not the object of their manipulation. When I stopped taking it personally, suddenly the hold it had over me lessened. And it's not like we were the only family to lose someone to fratricide, or the only family that had been given a less-than-honest story. Ours might have been the most highly publicized case, but unfortunately it wasn't the only one by a long shot.

Pat had joined the Army and yet not believed in the Iraq War. In the same way, I didn't agree with everything the military did but I saw its great purpose and potential. I saw a shared sense of values and character in the men and women who volunteered to serve that inspired me. Service members choose a difficult road, and regardless of where our system is today, the military is something that people should value and take pride in.

For all these reasons, I wanted to speak for military families, but first I had to conquer my lifelong fear of public speaking. This fear had held me back in life, from the time I had stood shaking in front of my high school class, tightly clenching my notes. And now my fear was certainly holding the Pat Tillman Foundation back, because I wasn't able to take advantage of the many speaking requests we'd received to educate people about the work we were doing.

I had assented to one appearance, and it hadn't gone well. Alex and I were invited to speak at the Clinton School of Public Service, and it was too good an opportunity to pass up. I spoke for only a minute or two, and my role was really just to introduce Alex, who did the heavy lifting. My couple of minutes in the spotlight were painful, my voice halting, and I resolved to get some training.

Alex had a friend in San Jose who worked for a public speaking company. At the time, I had no idea such a thing even existed. I figured some people were just naturally gifted in front of a crowd, and others, like me, were doomed to struggle through. The company worked mainly with CEOs and business speakers, but I decided to attend one of their training sessions to see if it might help. The company was located in a corporate office center in San Jose. I arrived early for my daylong session, and I made my way to the conference room, where a dozen businesspeople were arranged around the table.

A folder of information sat at each spot, and I flipped through mine nervously, waiting for the class to begin.

Our instructor, Melissa, inspired confidence from the moment she walked in the room. A petite brunette, she was poised to perfection. I wondered if one day of working with her could give me even a sliver of those skills. She gave us a brief overview of the day. We would each give a short presentation, which would be videotaped. Then, together, we'd watch the videos, critique the performances, and try again using techniques and methods the instructors suggested. My stomach dropped. The thought of watching myself on tape was as nerve-racking as the idea of getting up in front of this small crowd to speak. And I couldn't imagine sitting politely while *others* critiqued my performance.

"So, let's begin," Melissa said. "Any volunteers?"

The guy next to me raised his hand.

"Great, then we'll go around the table clockwise."

That meant I'd be next. I started to sweat and barely listened to the presentation the guy gave about the environmental advantages of his company's product. What was I going to say? I hadn't prepared for this. I wanted to run out of the room. When my turn came, I went up in front of the room with a few notes I'd jotted down about the foundation and our work with veterans and education. My hands were shaking and I could tell my voice was, too. I had an intense urge to cry but quickly got through my speech and sat down.

We went through everyone's presentations, then took a little break before moving on to the next step of watching the videos. During the break, one of the speaking company's owners, Mary, came up to me and introduced herself. She'd been in the back of the room, quietly observing. She looked to be in her midfifties and had kind eyes and an easy way about her.

"I know this must be difficult for you," she said in a motherly way that made me relax for the first time all morning. "You've been through so much.

"Your presentation is a little different from the other executives here," she added. "I realize it's very personal, but that's what also makes it powerful. Why don't we go into my office and we can work together one-on-one for the rest of the day?"

I was grateful for her kindness and willingness to help, and the thought of not having to suffer through a group examination was instantly appealing. I was a little embarrassed about the need for special attention but quickly got over it as I followed her to her office.

"You're at a place right now where you're nervous and stressed about getting up and speaking," Mary said once we'd settled in. "The techniques are things you can learn and perfect, but what you need to realize first is that you have something powerful and important to say."

We worked intently for the rest of the afternoon. We talked about Pat, the foundation, and what I most wanted people to know. She helped me see that I could share my story with people but still maintain comfortable boundaries. I left that day feeling much better, but the real test came several weeks later, at my next public appearance.

The foundation was holding its year-end dinner, an event that celebrated our scholars and brought together the community of donors and people who had supported the organization over the years. I practiced my speech all afternoon, talking to myself as I paced around my hotel room. Thinking back to my jitters before the Clinton School talk, I felt more prepared and optimistic that this experience would be better.

When it was finally time to step out onto the stage, I took a deep breath and started my memorized remarks. Being up there was almost an out-of-body experience; I was disconnected. Then, a few minutes in, something happened. I became instantly aware that *I* was up in front of a crowd. I heard a voice inside my head say, *Wow, this is not that bad.* But that little break in concentration threw me off autopilot, and I became acutely aware of all the eyes looking up at me. I took a moment to look down at my notes, which I had brought just in case, and tried to steady myself. I glanced at my notes several more times and skipped over a large section I had meant to include. Though not a complete success, the speech was better than any I'd given, and I tried not to chastise myself too much for not being perfect. Like every skill in life, with practice and in time, it would become better.

Public speaking was a huge hurdle to overcome, but

it was not by any means the only one. Logistically, running the foundation was difficult, because I was traveling back and forth between Los Angeles and Arizona, which made it harder for me to meet people and make a life for myself in Los Angeles. And though I'd supervised people in previous jobs, it was the first time I was the boss. Some of my employees were much older than I was, and I had to learn that though I wanted a friendly atmosphere, I couldn't be buddies with everyone. I drew on qualities of my former bosses that I'd liked, and tried to emulate them, tried to be in tune with my employees, giving them the structure and guidance they needed to do their jobs well, but enough flexibility that they'd feel empowered. There were many elements to running the foundation, and I'd never run a business before. I now oversaw personnel, fund-raising, operations, communications, scholar selection, everything. I needed to spearhead our vision and strategy while making sure that we had office space and that everyone's paychecks were signed. We'd get requests to partner with organizations, and staff would look to me and ask, "What do you want to do?" The truth was I had no idea. I worried incessantly about making the right decisions, and it took me months to realize there wasn't really a wrong decision. I just needed to conduct business the way I thought it should be done.

Emotionally the job was difficult, as well. There were still the questions, still the outpouring of sympathy.

Though almost four years had passed, and I was doing better than ever, the foundation had somehow thrust me back into the role of widow. I didn't see myself that way, but others did. I was constantly approached by people who would say things like "I'm so sorry about what happened to you." They were very nice, well-meaning comments by nice, sympathetic people. But it's awkward so many years later. It's hard when someone is looking at you with pity to respond with "Thanks. So, where are you from?"

I encountered misconceptions almost daily in my work for the foundation. Once after I'd given a presentation to potential donors, a businessman in attendance took me aside and said I was totally different from what he'd thought I'd be, and the foundation was totally different. I'm not sure what he'd expected—an old woman, dressed in black, who frowned all the time and cried at the drop of a hat?

Five minutes into a conversation with another group of potential donors, one said, "You're so young. Aren't you going to move on? How long are you going to do this?" As if my involvement in the foundation was about my personal grief. Even my dad said to me that he wasn't sure it was good for me to run the foundation, that he worried it would keep me down. But it wasn't like that. I wasn't going around crying each day as I held up photos of Pat, trying to make people feel compelled to do something because of their sympathy and guilt. That wasn't me at all, and that wasn't my message. The foundation started because of Pat, but it wasn't about him so much as it was about the spirit of service he'd instilled in me and in others he'd been close to. But still, I'd constantly be asked, "So what was he like?" and "Why did he enlist?" Questions that made me want to snap, "None of your damn business." I wanted people to focus on the work the foundation was doing to help this generation of veterans get an education.

It was wearing on me, so much so that I thought about getting out. Alex and Christine repeatedly checked in to see how I was faring, and so did Ben, who had been on the board of the foundation from the beginning.

"Honestly, I don't know about this," I told Ben one day when we met for lunch. "I'm starting to think this was a bad idea and that I should just quit."

"Yeah?" he said. "Why?"

In a rush of pent-up frustration, I told him about all the questions, all the people who just didn't get it, about how upset it still made me when people tried to mythologize Pat, and how aggravating it was that people couldn't see past him to the good work we were doing. "And why does everybody think it's okay to ask me when I'm going to get remarried and have kids, yet no one asks Beth?" I asked, referring to one of our administrators, who was forty-one and single.

"Marie," Ben said gently. "When you're putting yourself out there in a public role, people are going to want

something from you. It's part of the deal, and it's probably not going to change."

"So then maybe it's not right for me."

"Maybe not," he said. He was thoughtful a moment,
then added, "But you also have to consider that you're
good at your job, and that we're doing really good work,
that we're helping people. I'm not saying you shouldn't
walk away, but you have to consider both sides." He reminded me about the thank-you card we'd just received
from a couple we'd helped. The husband had been injured
in Iraq, and we were providing funding for his wife to go
back to school so she could support the family now that
the husband wasn't well enough to work.

"But I don't want to pressure you at all," Ben said, realizing it seemed like he was. I understood. He was just
trying to illuminate all sides of the issue. "No one is in
your situation but you."

Ben helped me see that if I left the foundation, I'd
be mad at myself for not getting past the roadblocks. In
certain lights, they seemed surmountable enough. I just
needed to find a way to control the direction of conversations so that the questions didn't get to me as much.
Again, it came down to perspective and whether I could
change mine. A line in *Self-Reliance* I'd returned to again
and again was "Good and bad are but names very readily
transferable to that or this; the only right is what is after my constitution, the only wrong what is against it."
I wanted to continue my work with the foundation and

still move on with my life, and I started to believe I could do both.

The next event I attended after my lunch with Ben was a gathering for Millennial veterans in Los Angeles, at which I was asked to speak. The conference was designed to encourage young veterans to use their leadership skills and experience to continue to give back to their communities. I wanted to let these veterans know that the Pat Tillman Foundation was stepping in to help the next generation, and I wanted hopefully to inspire them to continue their dedication to service in or out of uniform. The meeting was held in a hotel conference facility that felt rather impersonal, but the crowd was in good spirits and seemed excited to be there.

Before I went onstage, a tall, young, dark-haired guy came up to me. He played college football and had followed Pat's career at ASU and with the Cardinals. "Mrs. Tillman," he said. "Thank you for coming today. I hope you don't mind me asking, but I've wondered for a long time why Pat did what he did. Will you be going into that during your speech?"

"Yes," I said. "I will."

———

"Seven years ago," I said when I stepped up to the podium, "Pat and I started a journey together when he enlisted. Like all of you, we believed that it was our responsibility to do something for our community, and that we wanted to live our lives in a way that stood behind that value. I am continuing on that journey today."

I went on for a bit about the work of the foundation; then I opened it up for questions, the part of the presentation that always filled me with dread. "Mrs. Tillman." A hand rose in the crowd. "How did you feel when Pat enlisted? You were just newlyweds. Weren't you mad?"

"It's difficult to be a military spouse," I said, honestly answering her question while turning the conversation to the global issues I wanted to discuss. "I remember going in to work, and sitting through meetings where everyone was stressed out about a deadline, and thinking, 'My husband's in Iraq. Who cares about the deadline?' It felt like I was living on an alien planet or something. It's lonely, it's frightening. You have to learn how to do everything for yourself, and in my case, I was far from family and friends, and felt isolated. Military families need support, just as I needed support. And too often, they don't get it."

The speech marked a shift in what I was willing to discuss, and in the control I was able to take of the situation. I shared more than I ever had before about how I felt, but I focused on the feelings I was comfortable sharing. Almost as soon as I changed the tenor of my responses, I started seeing a difference in the people around me. More and more people approached me to say that they were military wives having a tough time, and that they related to my speech and me. One young woman came up to me and said she'd recently lost her spouse, and wanted to know what advice I had for her. I told her I thought grieving was an individual experience, without one remedy or solution, but that she should try to trust her gut and be confident that she would know what was best for her.

I took a lot of strength from the connections I now saw I was able to forge with others. After Pat died, I had sought out stories about people who had also been touched by tragedy. I couldn't read enough of their accounts of their difficult experiences, and how they'd overcome them. These were people who understood. And now I could be that person who understood. And I saw, too, that while my mask of privacy had given me control, sharing myself with others gave me power. But it had taken time and perspective to get to this place. I never could have done it in the first few years.

In what was perhaps the most unexpected connection, I was approached in the office one day by one of the women who had worked for the foundation for several years. Marcy and I were friendly but hadn't gotten to know each other well. I knew that she'd struggled to overcome breast cancer in her late twenties, but we hadn't really talked about it. I didn't want to pry, and she didn't offer much information about the experience. But on this day, as we were sitting in her office, chatting, she said, "You know, Marie,

I've always felt like we share something important in common."

"Yeah?" I said.

"Yeah. I mean, I know our experiences were really different, but we both went through a crisis at around the same age."

"You're right," I said. "I guess I hadn't thought about that before."

"It changes you," Marcy continued. "It's why I wanted to work at the foundation, to do something important with my life. Somehow when you go through something like we did, you just want your life to be significant, you know?"

I saw refrains of Marcy's observation all over the nonprofit world once I started looking. And nonprofit or not, stories abound about people who suffer a tragedy and go on to devote their lives to a greater cause. It was certainly a large part of why I was involved in the foundation. Perhaps it's so common it's clichéd. But really, who cares? Because at the end of the day, regardless of why we were all there, we had decided to do something worthwhile, which in the end was the only thing that mattered. And as I stood among people like Marcy, focused on making the world a better place, I saw the embodiment of Pat's world vision. I'd returned to the place I'd been when Pat had enlisted: holding hands with others, looking out on the world, ready to get to work.

CONCLUSION

"The first thing I saw as I walked off the plane was gorgeous, jagged, snow-covered mountain peaks."

Pat wrote that in a letter to me, dated April 9, 2004, just thirteen days before he was killed in the beautiful land he described. Since that month in 2004, I had felt an almost inexplicable pull to visit Afghanistan. Through the years I had explored many avenues in hopes of visiting this mysterious land, but I couldn't safely and reasonably find my way.

Then one day a way found me, in the form of the United Service Organizations (USO). After Pat's death, the NFL had generously donated money in his honor to the USO, who built the Pat Tillman Memorial USO Center at Bagram Airfield in Afghanistan. The USO was putting together a goodwill tour and asked me if I would like to go along to see the center. I said yes immediately.

"How long are you going to be there?" Christine quizzed me over the phone when I told her.

"Not very long—I think I'll only be in Afghanistan a day or two."

"What are you going to do there?"

"I don't know—they're sending a whole itinerary. I'll talk to people, take it all in."

"Is it safe?"

"Yes, relatively. They wouldn't have let me come along if not. Do you really think they'd want *that* kind of PR hanging over them?"

"No, I guess not," Christine said. "I think it's great, I do. I guess I just wonder what you're looking for there. It might be really hard for you."

She was right and wrong at the same time. I wasn't looking for closure, which is what she meant. I didn't anticipate that by seeing where Pat had died and seeing the center in his honor, I'd all of a sudden have a new acceptance of the loss. But she was right that it might be hard. Through my work with the foundation, I'd grown used to seeing men and women in uniform again, but it was one thing to attend meetings and fund-raisers on US soil, and another altogether to be thrust into the middle of their action, to be surrounded by military protocol again. But the immersion was also one reason I felt it was important to go. Since I was advocating for veterans at home, I felt like I needed a glimpse of their experiences abroad.

My alarm clock went off at four a.m., starting the long trek from Los Angeles to Afghanistan. It was still dark outside and I was quite cozy in bed, but I jumped up, eager to get going. I took a short flight from Los Angeles to Dallas, where I met up with the rest of the traveling group. The headliners were Gary Sinese and his Lt. Dan Band. Gary had received an Oscar nomination for playing the memorable Lieutenant Dan in the film *Forrest Gump*, and then years later matched the character name with his skills playing the bass and his passion for helping the USO. His band frequently performed for the military and for charities. I admired his generosity and commitment and immediately bonded with his troupe. Our group made a brief overnight stop at Landstuhl Regional Medical Center in Germany—the largest military hospital outside the United States—then boarded our flight to Kabul.

I stepped aboard the C-17 military transport and was overwhelmed by the size of the plane. It was a behemoth. It was hollowed out for cargo, with only two rows of airline seats. A few of us lucky ones got a seat, while the rest of the group lined the sides of the aircraft, trying to get comfortable in the flip-down seats. Some took to sleeping on the floor or put together makeshift beds on top of the cargo. The overnight flight took around ten hours, because we had to fly around Iran instead of taking the more direct route over it.

There were no windows on the plane, so I couldn't see any of Afghanistan until we landed at the US base in Kabul. I disembarked eagerly, excited to see the mountains Pat had described surrounding us, but was greeted instead by a thick mist that obscured the scenery. We were ushered into the mess hall, where breakfast had been prepared for us and the group of soldiers assigned to the Kabul base. I wasn't exactly expecting the rustic tents of *M*A*S*H* but was pleasantly surprised to see a long table lined with silver serving dishes, all of which were filled to the brim with eggs, bacon, toast, pancakes—more food than we could possibly eat. I loaded up my plate with pancakes, got some much-needed coffee, and sat toward the end of the long table.

A soldier was sitting to my right, and I introduced myself. He recognized the Tillman name and grasped what I was doing there.

"Hey, thanks for coming," he said. He had dark hair and an equally dark expression on his face. He didn't look angry, just distraught.

"How long have you been over here?" I asked.

"Just arrived," he said. He was quiet a minute, then looked away from his eggs and into my face. "Sorry," he said. "I'm just kind of upset. It was pretty hard to leave my kid."

With a few more gentle prods, I learned that his son was sixteen, and that he was a single dad.

"This is an important time in his life, you know?" he said. "And it was really tough for him when I left."

The complicated expression on his face, of both duty and guilt, was one I immediately recognized.

"You know," I said, "it was always hard for me to send Pat off, too. I was equally proud and terrified." I wanted this man to understand that while his family was certainly struggling without him, it was a burden that was carried with pride. Though I had tried to make our separations easier, of course Pat knew how hard it was for me, and was aware of the risks involved. He grappled with guilt for leaving me alone so much, fearing what would happen to his family if he was killed. I wanted to instill in this soldier the same confidence that as hard as it was, he was doing a great thing.

Soon our time allotted for breakfast was over, and I wished the soldier well and said a hesitant good-bye. He smiled and waved, and while I wasn't sure I'd made him feel better, we had at least connected in some minor way. At least he'd heard sympathy from someone who had been there, and that alone I hoped had some value, even if it was small in comparison to the miles and months of distance he was facing.

———

My group boarded a twenty-minute flight to Bagram, a trip that might easily have been taken by car if the threat of improvised explosive devices (IEDs) and attacks hadn't been so real. When it was originally built, the Bagram base housed around six thousand soldiers; at the time of my visit, Bagram's population was closer to thirty thousand. Once we landed, I went straight over to see the base's USO center. The Tillman memorial center looked like a little ski lodge and had a lodge's kitschy warmth to it. Open twenty-two hours a day, it provided Internet, movies, food, phones, and a badly needed sense of home for the thousands of soldiers who lived at Bagram and those who passed through.

The little lodge had just opened for the day twenty minutes before my arrival and yet was already overflowing with people. They relaxed in recliners, played video games, and had even spilled over onto the floor. A sweet staff member, aware of my arrival, graciously showed me around and explained what goes on at the center. As she introduced me to the people hanging out there, I sensed a heightened sensitivity to my presence. The soldiers around me seemed not quite sure what to expect or how I would act. It reminded me of the days soon after Pat had been killed, when everyone walked on eggshells—unsure if I might crack. I smiled as brightly as I could for as long as I could, hoping to put them at ease, to let them know how much I appreciated their service.

That night Gary and the Lt. Dan Band performed a two-hour show, full of music that kept the crowd singing and dancing. Just offstage, I had a great view of the crowd and smiled as I watched a young female soldier singing along up front. At one point during the show, Gary called all the women up onstage. I was transfixed as those women, some really more like young girls, swayed to the music, weapons slung across their backs. While they could get away from the war for a few hours to listen to some music, the weapons served as an ominous reminder of the reality of our surroundings. Watching the soldiers all rock out to the music, I was reminded of the feeling I'd had right after Pat had enlisted and we'd moved to Washington. I had been proud of him, and I was now proud of *them*. The men and women I met reminded me of what had been at the core of Pat's decision to serve, the purity of it all before lies and congressional hearings made me grow cynical and suspicious.

When the show was over, we drove back to our sleeping area to rest up for our long return trip in the morning. Soon after I got to my room, I heard a knock on the door. I opened it to see the general who had been acting as host for our contingent.

"Good evening, Mrs. Tillman. Sorry to disturb you, but I wanted to talk to you about something." The look in his eye and his restless movements suggested he was nervous. "Your flight tomorrow is a human remains flight." He looked at me intently for a moment, then added, "You'll be bringing the body of a young Special Forces soldier back home with you."

"Oh," I said. "Oh, okay."

"I just want to be sensitive to your feelings," the general added. "I want to be sure you're okay with it. If you're not, we can delay the remains flight."

"No, no," I said. "Absolutely no need." I remembered the intensity with which I had awaited Pat and Kevin's flight to Dover nearly six years earlier. I would never want a grieving family to have to wait a moment longer on my account.

"There will be a brief ceremony right before you take off. If you would like to attend..." His voice trailed off.

"Yes," I said. "Yes, of course."

Early the next morning, we loaded into a black SUV and made the short drive to the tarmac. The sun wasn't up yet, but as we pulled up, I saw light from the open door of the back of the plane. An array of soldiers had already assembled to say good-bye to one of their own. Since the deceased had been in the Special Forces, the guys he'd served with all had beards and scruffy appearances to make them look more like Afghans, and they were all in BDUs, or camouflage. A few were openly crying.

This is what they did for Pat, I thought. *This is how he left Afghanistan.* The soldiers stood at attention, forming two lines to make an aisle through which the coffin would be carried. Before we got out of the car, the general turned around and told us the young soldier's name and where he was from. Then he said, "Married, no kids."

I stood close to the general and tried to follow his lead through the ceremony, but *Married, no kids* echoed in my head. I heard the general's line in my head again and again and ached for his wife. I remembered all too clearly those first days after hearing Pat had been killed, the waiting for him to finally come home. As I stood in the cold, dark, misty morning, tears slid down my face, the warmth of them mixing with the cold drops of rain that had started to fall. The coffin was loaded onto the plane. A chaplain said a few words, and one at a time the soldiers walked onto the aircraft and knelt at the coffin to pay their last respects.

I boarded the plane when the time came, buckled in, and closed my eyes through takeoff. *Married, no kids.* I couldn't stop thinking about what that young widow had ahead of her—the funeral and then the months of numbness, the shock she'd encounter when the numbness wore off, the decisions she'd have to make, the ways she'd have to move forward despite what was lost.

As I had suspected, the trip to Afghanistan did not deliver closure. When it comes to grief, there's no such thing. There's no such thing as a nice, tidy ending where the widow feels a brave, strong resolve, where she looks out at the land and the water beneath her and feels at peace with the world. Grief is messy; grief is complicated; grief is in many ways unending. I knew I would miss Pat every day of my life. I knew I would have low periods again. But I felt grateful that I wasn't that young widow, just starting the journey. And I felt grateful that maybe, in some small way, I could help her.

Epilogue

Pat's last letter to me is tucked away now, among many letters we wrote to each other, in a shoe box in the closet of my house. I haven't pulled it out in a long time, but I've long since memorized it. Of all the letters from Pat through the years, from the one he wrote from juvenile hall to the one scribbled from Afghanistan envisioning the children we'd have someday, it's his "just in case" letter that I'm most grateful for and that more than anything has seen me through these past few years. And though it sits in a nondescript shoe box in a closet, it is precisely because of how valuable it is that I keep it there, safe and secure.

I've come far since those days after I first read the letter. In many ways I'm a different person—stronger, independent, more self-assured. I can travel alone. I can make decisions alone. I can kick myself out of a funk, and I can contribute of my own volition to the world. I no longer feel conflicted about having a good time. If I'm meeting people for drinks, I don't attach deep meaning to the color of clothing I choose to wear, or worry what I'll say if someone asks me if I'm single.

Recently, I spent a month in Laos, where I was a volunteer English teacher. As part of the conversation practice, students asked me again and again, "Are you married?"

"I was," I repeated with student after student, "but my husband died."

"Oh," the student would say. Then she would move on to the next question. "And what does your father do?"

The questions didn't bother me. I was much more affected by being there, in a beautiful Laotian village, helping young girls improve their English so they would have better job opportunities, than by any questions asked about my past, or by any answers I gave.

I realized in Laos that although I was moving forward, I didn't have to leave Pat behind. I could carry him with me in the memories of our life together, the interactions that have left a permanent imprint on my soul. Loving and losing Pat changed me. And while I wish he were still here, I don't want to turn back the clock and be who I was when he was alive. I like who I am now.

I am finally happy with the work I'm doing, the mark I'm striving to make. Spending my days helping others feels worthwhile and meaningful, and I've met countless wonderful people along the way...including one person more memorable than any other.

It was during a recent trip to Chicago, where I'd traveled to meet with one of the foundation's new board members, Ian, and some of Ian's friends and colleagues. The purpose of the meeting was to spread awareness about the foundation's work, with the hope of garnering some support in the Midwest. We had a dinner scheduled the night I flew in, and after a delayed flight and a long trip, I was not in the mood to socialize. I entered the restaurant wishing I'd be back at my hotel and in bed as soon as possible. But when Ian introduced me to his friend Joe, my mood significantly lifted and I immediately forgot all about the delayed flight and lack of sleep.

The only word I could think of to describe Joe was beautiful—not his physical being (though with his blue eyes and slightly crooked smile, he was adorable) but his spirit. He had a beautiful spirit that radiated from within and an easy way about him that instantly attracted me. But as we talked I quickly sensed that parts of his life had not been so easy.

We chatted for hours, all but ignoring our dinner company. Somehow I just knew that he got it, that he saw through the story that surrounded me, and just saw *me*. I could have stayed there and talked with him all night. Something almost mystical happened at that restaurant. Although our conversation ranged from pop culture to the minutiae of our daily lives, what we were communicating was that while we had both weathered our share of disappointment and loss, we remained hopeful and open to life.

Before Joe and I said good-bye, we made plans to meet for dinner the following week, when he would be in Los Angeles on business. I didn't know where this chance meeting with a kind and interesting man would lead, and I realized that wasn't what was important. What mattered was that I was being open to all of life's possibilities, and no matter what happened, I'd be okay; I'd been bruised, but what I felt that night proved I had not been broken.

I returned to my hotel in a happy daze, thinking about all that had happened during the past six years, how quickly life could bring you to your knees or make you soar, the challenges, the delight, the wonder of it all. Life would always be dynamic, unpredictable, and messy, but that reality no longer scared me. I had learned to take things as they came, to embrace life's joys and challenges. Despite everything, I had managed to stay open. Open to life, open to love.

As I consider this chapter in my life and move forward to the next, I find myself thinking about Pat's final letter to me and how the familiar words have now taken on new meaning. In the military, it's fairly common to write a "just in case" letter like the one Pat left for me, just as it's common for critically ill people to leave words and messages behind for those they love. It's like wrapping the people you care about in a warm winter coat when you know you can't be there personally to protect them from next season's cold spells. Since Pat died, I've thought a lot about what people leave behind, the mark we all make just by being here; big or small, it's up to us.

When Pat asked me to live, he didn't mean just that I should travel and have fun, although that was certainly part of it. He also meant that there's a weight to all of our lives, and he didn't want me to be frivolous with mine. It was a tragedy that Pat's life—while lived fully—was cut short. But it's also a tragedy to live a long life that isn't meaningful. Our lives should have depth, which means pushing ourselves out of our comfort zones and not taking the easy way out all the time. That is the only way to really live.

It has taken years, but I am at that point now. I am truly, deeply living.

THE PAT TILLMAN FOUNDATION

Shortly after Pat's death in 2004, with a group of close friends and family, I started the Pat Tillman Foundation. Our mission is to invest in military veterans and their spouses through educational scholarships, building a diverse community of leaders committed to service to others. I am proud to say that since inception, through the generous support of individuals and organizations nationwide, over $4 million has been invested in men and women committed to a life of service, both in and out of uniform. I invite you to take a moment to view the interactive Scholar Map online at **www.pattillmanfoundation.org** to learn more about the Tillman Military Scholars who are making a difference in your community.

Below are just a few of the many ways you can get involved:

Run, Walk, Honor.

Join 35,000 participants, volunteers, and spectators from throughout the United States at Pat's Run, the foundation's signature annual fund-raiser. Learn more about the event and the various ways you can participate or volunteer at www.patsrun.com.

Commit. Challenge. Support.

The Pat Tillman Foundation is honored to be recognized as an Official Charity Partner with guaranteed entries to participate in some of the most prestigious marathons in the world, including the ING New York City Marathon, the Bank of America Chicago Marathon, and the Marine Corps Marathon. By becoming a member of Team Tillman, individuals can earn gear and raise funds at these events and in conjunction with any race or athletic event nationwide.

Give. Donate. Invest.

Invest in veterans and military families today by making a tax-deductible donation to support the Tillman Military Scholars program.

Stay Informed.

Become a Fan on Facebook—Pat Tillman Foundation (Official), follow us on Twitter @pattillmanfnd, and stay up to date on recent Tillman Military Scholars' achievements and foundation news and events at www.pattillmanfoundation.org.

If *The Letter* has inspired you to live a little more, give a little more, or just be a little more, please join me at www.marietillman.com